THE MANAGEMENT SKILLS BOOK

The Management Skills Book

Conor Hannaway and Gabriel Hunt

Gower

HD
31
H316
1992

© Conor Hannaway 1992

Published by
Gower Publishing Company Limited
Gower House
Croft Road
Aldershot
Hants GU11 3HR
England

Gower Publishing Company Limited
Distributed in the United States by
Ashgate Publishing Company
Old Post Road
Brookfield
Vermont 05036
USA

British Library Cataloguing in Publication Data
Hannaway, Conor
  The management skills book.
  I. Title II. Hunt, Gabriel
  658.4

ISBN 0 566 07283 1

Printed and bound in Great Britain by
Billing and Sons Limited, Worcester.

HF 25320578
12/28/94 OH

Contents

Preface   xi
Acknowledgements   xiii
How to use this book   xv

1   **Personal effectiveness**   1

    The successful manager   3
    Defining your job   5
    Agreeing performance requirements   7
    Getting along with your boss   8
    Managing your time   9
    A time management system   10
    Time-wasters   16
    Analysing your work   18
    Coping with the paperwork jungle   20
    Effective reading   21
    Improving your memory   23
    The nature of stress   24
    Managing stress   27
    A relaxation exercise   29
    Management and the life stages   31
    Managing your career   33
    Assessing a career move   35

2 **Leadership**   37

    The manager as leader   39
    Choosing a leadership style   40
    Power   42
    Organizational politics   44
    Effective work groups   45
    Developing teamwork   47
    Conflict between groups   49
    Managing conflict   51
    Staff training and development   53

3 **Planning**   57

    Making plans   59
    The elements of a plan   60
    Barriers to planning   62
    Making plans effective   64
    Critical path analysis   66
    Managing change   69
    Overcoming resistance to change   71
    Forcefield analysis   75

4 **Recruitment and selection**   77

    Job design   79
    Job descriptions   81
    The person specification   83
    Before the interview   84
    Recruitment advertising   85
    During the interview   86
    The seven-point interview plan   88
    Types of question and their use   90
    Useful interview questions   92
    After the interview   94
    Final selection and job offer   95
    Checking references   96
    Giving feedback to non-successful candidates 98

5 **Managing employee performance** 99

Inducting new employees 101
Giving training instruction 102
Defining performance requirements 103
Giving instructions 106
Improving employee performance 108
Delegating 110
Giving performance feedback 113
Recognizing progress 115
Recognizing above-average performance 116
Managing the poor performer 117
Performance appraisal 119
Rewarding performance 121
Discussing a salary change 123
Coaching 124
Career counselling 126

6 **Employee relations** 129

Managing employee relations 131
Rules about rules 134
The disciplinary meeting 135
Disciplinary penalties 138
Grievance procedure 139
Grievance meetings 140
Counselling 141
Management by walking about 142

7 **Problem solving and decision making** 145

Problem solving 147
Types of problem 148
Cause-and-effect diagrams 149
Pareto analysis 152
Creative problem solving 155
Group problem solving 157
Brainstorming 158
Nominal group technique 160
Groupthink 161
Avoiding procrastination 163

Being decisive   164
Decision tree technique   165

8 **Meetings**   171

Taking the chair   172
Controlling a meeting   174
Reaching a consensus   176
Participation at meetings   177
Assessing a meeting   179
Preparing minutes   181
Leading a discussion group   182
A conference checklist   183

9 **Communication**   185

Managing the communication process   187
Planning your communication   189
Barriers to communication   190
Seven rules for effective communication   192
Being assertive   194
Non-verbal behaviour   196
Developing verbal fluency   198
Listening   200
Do's and don'ts for better writing   202
Report writing   203
The elements of a report   205
Selling your report   207
Writing a business letter   208
Writing a letter of complaint   209
Replying to complaints   210

10 **Presentation**   211

Preparing a presentation   213
The magic envelope technique   215
Presenting at short notice   217
Delivering a presentation   218
Closing a presentation   219
Visual aids   220

A formula for using visual aids   221
Using the overhead projector   222
Introducing a speaker   224
Proposing a vote of thanks   225
Speaking at a company competition   226
Opening an event   227
Presenting an award   228
The retirement presentation   229
Accepting an award   230

Preface

If you are a practising manager, this book is for you. You will find that it is different from most books on management. It is designed to answer your need for support in your day-to-day work as a manager. You will find in it very little discussion of theories and concepts. This is deliberate. We are not suggesting that the underlying theories and concepts are not important. They are. But they have their place, and that place is not at the practising manager's desk.

In the course of running many hundreds of training programmes for managers and executives from around the world we have identified a common feature. After all the new ideas and concepts have been discussed and the arguments are over, these managers and executives want to reach some conclusions about what they should do. They know that each situation is different, but they also know that, for each situation, there are certain principles which must be followed and actions which they should take. They don't want to have to run through all the old arguments. They want to know what the best practice is. This book is our response to their needs.

It consists of a series of brief guides to management action. The contents cover the most important parts of the manager's job, and the style is similar to a reference manual. It gives you all you need to know without burdening you with the technical details. You look it up, identify the best practice and apply it straight away. As you use the skills in this book you will get better at them. Some of the skills are quite complex and you may need training to be able to practise them effectively. Many of the skills are straightforward, and simply by following the appropriate guide you will be effective right away.

There is one thing which we have learned from the hundreds of managers with whom we have worked: every manager has a unique way of doing things, and that is alright. Different situations may call for different approaches. This makes the job of the manager more exciting and challenging. However, the underlying principles remain the same in any situation. The main differences tend to be in style and emphasis. When you practise your managerial skills, you can follow the best practice set out in this book, adapting it to your own style of management. Your distinctive style will make the results uniquely your own.

The search for best practice never ends. Research and practical experience both add to our knowledge in this regard. We welcome comments and feedback from readers and users of this book. Practising managers are ideally placed to let us know what has worked well and what can be improved. We thank you in anticipation of your involvement in this process.

Conor Hannaway
Gabriel Hunt

Acknowledgements

The format and style of this book are unique. The content is not. It is based on the best practice of effective managers. Our first thanks go to those managers with whom we have worked for sharing their experiences with us. We must also acknowledge the work of researchers, academics and trainers who helped to identify, clarify and prescribe many of the skills set out in this book. Their contribution to the evolution of management practice is often hidden behind the glow which surrounds the achievements of the successful manager.

The material in this book was originally prepared as part of a starter-kit for newly appointed managers entitled *Guide to Effective Management,* published by the Irish Management Institute. This package was so well received that existing managers looked for their copy. This book is our response. Accordingly, our thanks go to all the staff of the Institute who contributed to and supported the development of the starter-kit.

A number of people deserve special mention. Gerald Smyth was responsible for obtaining the funding for the project, and was an enthusiastic supporter throughout. Jenny Hayes was an indefatigable colleague whose good humour saw us through some difficult moments, especially as the print deadlines approached. Alex Miller and his wife Aine played a vital role in editing the manuscript and preparing it for publication. Our final thanks go to Malcolm Stern of Gower Publishing for his part in identifying the potential of the package as a working textbook for all managers.

The trials associated with being a writer are nothing compared with the tribulations of being married to one. Words cannot express the debt of gratitude owed to our wives, Sinead and Teresa, for their support, encouragement and perseverance during the eighteen months it took to produce the text.

Our thanks to you all.

CH
GH

How to Use this Book

This book is designed to help you in your daily work as a manager. It covers the key aspects of management – planning, leading, organizing and controlling both your own work and that of your subordinates. As a manager you do not have the time to read textbooks or lengthy articles whenever you start a new task. You need a reference manual which will quickly give you the information you need to act. Use this book as you would a car manual, referring to the appropriate section when the need arises.

The book is divided into ten sections, each section comprising a number of guides. Most of the guides take the form of one-page To Do lists, setting out the key actions required to complete a particular task. For example, the recruitment section contains guides to writing job descriptions, interviewing and checking references. The meetings section includes guides to chairing meetings, reaching consensus and writing minutes. Some guides contain, instead of a To Do list, information to explain the purpose of other guides in the section.

Follow these steps to get the best use from the manual:

— Become familiar with the layout and content of the manual by browsing through it.

— Keep it in a convenient place so that you can refer to it quickly.

— When you know you will be doing a type of work which you have never done before, read all the guides in the relevant section to get an overview of what is involved.

— Select the relevant guides. Use them to develop an action list of tasks to be completed. For example, if you are responsible for preparing a plan, review these guides:

— Elements of a Plan

— Barriers to Planning

— Making Plans Effective

— On other occasions a single guide will contain all the information you need; for example, to check a reference, or to hold a brainstorming session.

This manual gives you the knowledge to perform most managerial tasks. As you perform these tasks try to evaluate how well you do them. Ask for feedback from colleagues and subordinates so that you can improve your skills. Attend off-the-job training courses to develop fully those skills you use most frequently.

1 Personal Effectiveness

The first guide in this section sets out the characteristics of successful managers. The message is clear. Self-management is the key to success as a manager. Put another way, the most important person you have to manage is yourself. In this section there are 17 guides to help you to be both effective and efficient in your work. When you have mastered these, you have prepared yourself for the challenging task of managing other people.

The first step in managing yourself is to manage your work. To do this, you must have a clear understanding about what your job entails. When people are asked to describe their jobs, their description very often differs significantly from their boss's perception of the job. Frequently, they do not focus on the same areas. To be effective you must be sure that you are doing the right things. Firstly, you define your job by clarifying its purpose and the key work areas in which you are required to achieve results. Next you agree the standards of performance by which you will be measured with your boss. Finally, you set the context for your own work by developing an effective working relationship with your boss. The objective here is the development of an open, trusting and mutually supportive relationship.

Time management is an important part of being effective. It ensures that you spend your time on the right things, and that you make best use of this critical resource. The guides in this section provide a system to manage your time and to help you eliminate some of the most significant time wasters.

Managing yourself involves learning how to cope with the pressures of your job and the stress they put on your mind and body. The quality of your life both at work and at home will improve as you learn how to manage stress. You will also be able to support colleagues and subordinates who are under pressure at work.

The final guides in this section will enable you to manage your life through career planning, and will help you to assess one of life's most important decisions – the career move.

When you have mastered these skills and are able to demonstrate personal effectiveness, you will be in a good position to start thinking about managing the work of others.

The successful manager

Much research has been done into the careers of successful managers. A number of managerial skills, personal traits and values have been identified as important.

- Being productive (getting things done).

- Setting challenging goals for oneself.

- Fluency in expressing ideas.

- Being an assertive communicator.

- Technical competence.

- Team leading skills.

- Being loyal and supportive to management and colleagues.

- Having a positive approach to problems.

- Prepared to make sacrifices for career.

- Having a personal meaning in life.

On the other hand, a number of characteristics have been identified with careers which have ended prematurely.

- Specific performance problems.

- Poor interpersonal skills.

- Inability to adapt to boss's style.

- Failures in staff selection and development.

- Overmanaging.

- Failure to develop an effective team.

- Overdependence on support of another.

By following the guides to managerial action in this manual you will be able to examine the managerial skills issues highlighted in the research. The personality traits and values you must take care of yourself.

Defining your job

Most job descriptions list a series of activities which the job holder is expected to complete. A different approach puts the emphasis on what the job holder is expected to achieve. This approach emphasizes performance effectiveness. A three stage process is involved.

Establish objectives
Objectives are a statement of why the position exists. Sometimes there is a single objective for a position, more often a number. Here are examples of objectives for two managerial positions.

A sales manager might have three objectives:

- To increase sales revenue.

- To control costs.

- To run the office effectively.

A product manager might have a single objective:

- To increase revenue from sales of product X.

Define key result areas
Key result areas refer to those parts of the manager's work which are critical to achieving the objectives of his or her position.

A quality manager might have the objective 'to ensure product conformity to customer specifications. Key result areas might include:

- agreeing product specifications.

- instrument calibration.

- inspection.

- vendor certification.

Set goals
Goals are the standard by which managerial performance is measured. All performance can be measured in terms of quantity, quality, cost and time. In fact, all goals should include a time factor. Examples of goals are as follows:

- Increase sales of product X by 5% per quarter over the next 12 months.

- Reduce absenteeism to 4% by the end of July.

- Hire ten graduate engineers during quarter 1.

To set effective goals use the *SMART* formula. Ensure that goals are:

- Specific.

- Measurable.

- Attainable but challenging.

- Relevant.

- Time-orientated.

If you are working from a job description, develop objectives, key result areas and standards of performance for your job. Agree them with your manager.

Agreeing performance requirements

Job requirements change over time, and it is important that the requirements for your position be reviewed with your boss on a regular basis. Reviews should take place at least once a year, and six-monthly reviews are often necessary.

- Set a time with your boss when you can discuss the requirements of your position. For managerial jobs a few hours are normally necessary.

- Establish the objectives, and note any changes from previous objectives.

- Agree the key result areas which will meet these objectives.

- Determine the standard of performance required, and agree goals which help to meet business objectives.

- Record the objectives, key result areas and the agreed goals in writing, and send a copy to your boss.

- Fix a date for reviewing performance against goals.

Getting along with your boss

It is important to know how to get along well with your boss if you wish to be successful in your career. If you want to ensure things are done, you usually need to win the agreement of your own boss. In winning his or her approval, bear the following in mind:

- Aim for a good relationship.

- Be loyal.

- Bring your boss solutions rather than problems.

- Meet deadlines.

- Keep your boss informed when things are going right, and also when they are not going right.

- When your boss makes a mistake, don't rub it in.

- Don't be defensive. Accept his or her ideas and amendments to your proposals, if they make sense. If you are in the wrong, admit it. Better to admit a mistake than be found out.

- Never provoke confrontation in the presence of others.

- Time your approach to suit your boss's mood. Make sure that he or she has enough time before you raise a topic for discussion.

- Check on the precise terms of reference for any project before you begin it.

- You will get along best if you help him or her to succeed.

Managing your time

Time is the most critical resource you have. When time is used effectively, activities are planned and goals achieved. Research, however,
indicates that up to 50% of a manager's time is wasted on activities
which do not achieve meaningful results. Successful time management
has two aspects. It means spending time on the key result areas of your
position. It also involves the elimination of the most common time-
wasters to which every manager is subject.

There are six rules for effective time management:

- Use a time management system and stick to it. There is no one best
  system. Develop one which meets your needs. Success comes from
  adhering to it.

- Distinguish between effectiveness and efficiency. Effectiveness
  means doing the right things. Efficiency is doing things the right
  way. Be effective and efficient.

- Distinguish between urgent and important tasks. Even though a
  task is urgent it may not be important, and you should endeavour
  to get it out of the way as quickly as possible. Important tasks
  should be given the time they deserve.

- Try to spend more than half your time on proactive tasks, that is,
  tasks which you have planned to do in advance. In this way, the
  time spent reacting to situations will be reduced. Avoid the activity
  trap (being too busy to prioritize) and prevent yourself moving into
  crisis management.

- Develop plans for dealing with time-wasters.

- Review your progress regularly.

A time management system

Develop your own time management system, one that meets your needs and suits your way of doing things. One possible system involves annual, six-monthly, monthly, weekly and daily planning activities. Do a little planning often. Increase the amount of time you spend on your key result areas by scheduling proactive tasks.

A few guidelines will help you plan your time:

- Maintain a tasks list within your time management system. Every time a new task arises write it into the task list together with the date by which it must be finished (Figure 1.1).

- Routines make life easier. Develop routines such as opening and dealing with your mail first thing every morning.

- Develop routines for your weekly and daily time planning. Many managers like to do their weekly planning for the following week last thing on a Friday.

- Always leave unscheduled time to cope with emergencies, to meet colleagues and as an opportunity to think.

Annually
- Agree performance requirements with your boss.

- Complete a project activities calendar showing the start and finish times of all the main activities which you intend to accomplish in the coming year (Figure 1.2). Avoid the temptation to frontload into the first half of the year.

- Complete a job analysis exercise at least once a year.

- Agree job requirements with your subordinates.

Annual Project Calendar

Year _____

Name of Project	1	2	3	4	5	6	7	8	9	10	11	12	13	14	15	16	17	18	19	20	21	22	23	24	25	26	27	28	29	30	31	32	33	34	35	36	37	38	39	40	41	42	43	44	45	46	47	48	49	50	51	52

☐ Indicates the start of the project ◯   ☐ Indicates the end of the project X   ☐ Join the start and the end ◯–X

Figure 1.1
Annual Project Calendar

11

Date Received	Task	Finish Date

Figure 1.2
Task List

- Schedule dates when progress against job requirements can be reviewed.

Six-monthly
- Review of progress with boss and with subordinates.

- Revise, if necessary, key result areas and goals.

- Update project activities calendar.

Monthly
- Decide on key result areas for that month (Figure 1.3).

- Set goals for that month.

- Schedule activities to achieve goals.

Weekly
- Carry forward items not completed during previous week.

- Review tasks list to prioritize activities.

- Schedule activities, if possible, placing those to be completed that week early in the week.

- Leave enough time unscheduled to allow for emergencies, etc.

Daily
- Check diary for appointments.

- Prepare a To Do list (Figure 1.4).

- Prioritize activities to ensure that you attend to the most important tasks.

- Schedule a small amount of time to attend to urgent, but unimportant, tasks.

- Schedule, if necessary, informal activities such as 'managing by walking about'.

Date: _____

Key Result Area	Goals	Activities
1 _____		
2 _____		
3 _____		
4 _____		
5 _____		
6 _____		

Figure 1.3
Monthly Planner

Date_____

Appointments	Priorities	Telephone
7.30		
8.00		
8.30		
9.00		
9.30		
10.00		
10.30		
11.00		
11.30		
12.00		
12.30		
1.00		

Appointments	Notes
1.30	
2.00	
2.30	
3.00	
3.30	
4.00	
4.30	
5.00	
5.30	
6.00	
EVENING	

Figure 1.4
Things to do Today

Time-wasters

The worst time-waster is not to devote the greatest amount of your time to your key result areas. Use an effective time management system to eliminate that problem. There are, however, many other time-wasters. The most frequent are set down below, together with suggestions for dealing with them. Some are so important that they are dealt with in more detail in other parts of this book.

Telephone calls
When these occur during your most productive times they break your concentration and upset your train of thought. Tell your secretary or telephonist when you do not wish to take calls. Delegate routine enquiries and arrange a call back system for returning calls at a low priority time of your day.

The uninvited visitor
When this visitor walks into your office, stand up and walk towards him or her. Be polite and respond to quickly answerable questions. Do not offer a seat or sit down yourself. Explain that you are busy on an important task and suggest a more suitable time for a meeting. Walk towards the door.

Disorganized paperwork
Have a policy of handling each piece of paper once. File regularly.

Overcommitment
Being a willing worker very often results in overcommitment. Don't agree to take on too many tasks which are unimportant and which won't help you to achieve your goals. Learn to say 'No'.

Travel and waiting
Use this time for your reading. Long journeys are also good opportunities to catch up on paperwork. Build that time into your schedule. Keep

your time management system with you so that waiting can be put to good use.

Meetings

Attend essential meetings only, and ensure that these are conducted in a businesslike manner. Be prepared for the meeting, and insist that others are prepared as well. End meetings in a polite manner.

Poor communications

Whether you are delegating or contracting with others, poor communications waste time. Make sure that others know the When, Where, What and Why of the task. Check to make sure that you know what they want.

Bad timekeeping

Bad timekeeping, whether late starts, early finishes or prolonged breaks, are total wastes of time and should be strictly controlled.

Lack of energy

Personal energy levels rise and fall throughout the day and the week. Find out how your energy levels rise and fall. Schedule demanding tasks for your high energy times and complete your routine work during low energy times.

Poor health and lack of fitness

Poor health and condition can seriously affect all aspects of your life. Keep in shape with physically and mentally stimulating exercise. Eat a moderate and varied diet. Build in sufficient time for all aspects of your life, family, friends and other interests.

Analysing your work

As a manager you engage in four basic types of work:

- technical (your core specialism)

- administrative

- managerial

- non-productive

If you are, for example, a sales manager, technical work for you would be negotiating with a customer, administrative work would be checking the expenses of your sales reps, while managerial work would be setting objectives and goals, and motivating and coaching your reps. Non-productive time may be spent on personal business, in the cafeteria or chatting with colleagues. You will find it most revealing to complete this exercise.

- Keep an activity record over three typical days of the tasks you are engaged in. Mark them technical (T), administrative (A), managerial (M) or non-productive (NP).

- Use the time-log in Figure 1.5 to capture details of how you use your time in 15 minute intervals. Be sure to record all interruptions. Fill it in every hour.

- Decide whether you are spending enough time on managerial work and on your key result areas.

- Watch out for a tendency to gravitate to work you like doing.

19

This time log should be maintained for three **typical** days. Use it to find out exactly how you spend your time. Fill it in during the day.	Code
8.00	
8.15	
8.30	
8.45	
9.00	
9.15	
9.30	
9.45	
10.00	
10.15	
10.30	
10.45	
11.00	
11.15	
11.30	
11.45	
12.00	
12.15	
12.30	
12.45	
1.00	
1.15	
1.30	
1.45	
2.00	
2.15	
2.30	
2.45	
3.00	
3.15	
3.30	
3.45	
4.00	
4.15	
4.30	
4.45	
5.00	
5.15	
5.30	
5.45	
6.00	

Time Spent Technical(T)_____hrs   Administrative(A) _____hrs
Managerial(M)_____hrs   Non-productive(NP) _____hrs

Figure 1.5
Time Log

Coping with the paperwork jungle

Every piece of paper should have a home to go to. A manager's best friend is the wastepaper basket. Cope more effectively with the paperwork jungle by observing the following precepts:

- Force yourself to act on documents at once. Write or dictate an immediate answer. One method of correcting your tardiness is to mark the document with a red dot each time you look at it but fail to take action. Allow three red dots to accumulate, but no more. It is not always necessary to send a typed letter. Very often a handwritten reply on incoming correspondence is sufficient. Get a photocopy for your records and send the original back to the sender.

- Find a home for each piece of paper that crosses your desk. You can dump some, delay some in 'Parking lots' (but write on them the date on which you intend to deal with them), and delegate some to people more appropriate to deal with them. Keep a note of this for your own reference.

- Every morning, check your Parking lot file to see what documents are due to be dealt with on that day.

- Remember that the function of a filing system is not storage but retrieval. Have simple, clear and meaningful files. At least once a year go through your filing system and clear out all the documents that have become obsolete.

- Delegate the reading of non-essential/routine documents to others whenever you can, and ask them to send you any extracts and summaries personally relevant to you.

- Try to leave a clear desk every night.

Effective reading

Today's manager is expected to be well-read and up-to-date in the literature concerning his or her specialism. While it is not necessary to read everything more quickly, you should be able to read more effectively. Here are some hints to enable you to do this:

- Distinguish between reading for total understanding and merely obtaining an overall impression of what you read.

- Decide how much time you are going to spend on reading at a particular session. Stop when this is up. This practice puts a boundary on your reading and helps you to feel in control.

- Before you start reading a particular topic, review what you already know about that topic. A useful technique is to look up the topic heading beforehand in a reference book which will give you a useful bird's-eye view.

- Ask yourself: 'Why am I reading this material?' This helps you to read with a purpose. Set yourself a short list of questions that you want answered from the text. At the end of your reading ask yourself whether your queries have been answered in full.

- Skim through the material before you read it in depth in order to obtain an overall impression and to locate particular information. Do this by skimming through the contents list, the index, headings, illustrations, italics, underlinings, lists and the opening of paragraphs.

- Read summaries (if given) before reading the main text. With articles, read the beginning and the end first of all.

- Read critically. Are any facts incorrect or out of date? It is also useful to make notes/summaries in your own words having read the whole material. This aids in making your reading more active. Ask yourself: 'What's the message?' Do you agree with it?

- Make notes in the margin as you go along.

- Jot down main points at the beginning of the article or chapter. This device saves re-reading at a later stage.

- If you wish to practise speed reading from a page of text, reduce the number of your eye fixations, that is, the number of times your eyes stop to relax when reading a line of type from left to right. Practise fixing on two words at a time, then three words, and so on. Scoop the words up in bunches and as you read, keep your lips closed to avoid saying each word. Move your index finger or a pencil quickly down the page. Your attention is focused and your eyes move more quickly and smoothly along the line.

- Read sitting upright in a straight-backed chair and in good light. Relax your eyes during long reading periods by occasionally looking up and focusing on distant objects. Another way is to close them at intervals and cover them with your hands to produce total blackness.

Improving your memory

Your memory is like a muscle that needs to be stretched and exercised if you are to keep it in peak condition. Try not to overload your memory. Here are some hints to help you use your memory more effectively:

- Lighten your memory load by devising simple routines such as having a To Do list and a Remember to Bring list.

- Have a place for everything and keep everything in its place.

- Make visual associations. For example, when you park your car in a strange place look for something unusual near your car as a visual association. Put things you might forget next to something you cannot forget.

- Write a note on the bathroom mirror, put a knot in your handkerchief, leave your shoe in the middle of your bedroom floor, reverse the watch on your wrist.

- Carry a notepad and write notes on it during the day. This technique is also an important aid to creativity.

- To remember people's names, make sure you hear the name properly when someone is introduced to you. If you don't remember the name, ask for it to be repeated and then use it occasionally during the conversation. Link the name with some physical feature or other characteristic of the person.

The nature of stress

Most employees experience moderate degrees of work-related stress. This is good. It arises from the demands that employees' jobs place on them. Its absence could indicate that the job is undemanding and accordingly not challenging or interesting. Too much stress over a prolonged period is bad for employees. It has a negative impact on both performance and on employee job satisfaction. There are many instances of serious damage being caused by over-stressed employees, who themselves have suffered ill health and other disorders. Stress management is therefore important.

Monitor the extent to which your subordinates feel under stress in their jobs. Remember that each employee is affected differently by work demands, and that factors outside work can cause very great stress to employees. It makes sense to reduce work demands on employees who are under undue stress at work or at home. Some of the most common causes of stress are:

At work
- Changed duties/responsibilities.

- Lack of feedback on performance.

- Work overload.

- Role conflict.

- Role ambiguity.

- Poor training.

- Poor relationships.

- Uncertainty.

- Change in work hours or conditions.

At home
- Increased financial commitments.

- Gaining a new family member.

- Change in residence.

- Death of spouse/close friend.

- Major personal injury or illness.

- Marriage or divorce.

- Legal problems.

- Difficulties with family or friends.

The effects of stress
There are three identifiable phases reflecting the impact of acute stress on employees:

Phase one
Under acute stress employees respond with high levels of energy. They work extremely hard, skipping days off, holidays, etc. They have little time for their interests or their family. Eventually they become concerned at the continued acute level of stress and doubt their ability to continue to operate at that rate.

Phase two
This phase is characterized by an increasing level of discontent with the job demands. More and more anxiety and frustration arise. Employees feel unable to cope with the pressure and begin to distance themselves from the job and from the work of other employees. They begin to experience tiredness and resentment.

Phase three
This phase is characterized by a sense of failure on the part of the

employees. Work suffers from employee turnover, absenteeism, ill health and possibly drug dependence. Employees avoid work and social contact with colleagues and distance themselves emotionally from the organization.

Managing stress

Because of the impact of stress on job performance, it is important that you are aware of the degree of stress experienced by yourself and your subordinates. You should try to maintain stress at an appropriate level. Work demands should rise and fall giving employees an opportunity to recover.

Carry out a personal stress audit in order to identify the job factors that increase stress for you and your subordinates. Knowing what they are, you can then decide to do something about them. The audit should focus on the individual employees and how they are responding to sources of stress at work and at home.

Develop a *personal action plan*.

- Take work breaks every two hours.

- Practise relaxation techniques each day.

- Have a full medical check-up once a year.

- Get enough sleep.

- Watch your diet.

- Exercise regularly, four times a week.

- Discuss priorities for your life with your partner.

- Develop out-of-work hobbies.

- Pace yourself and manage your personal time more effectively in order to avoid time pressures.

- Seek job feedback from your boss at the end of all major projects and, at least once a year, have a full formal review.

A relaxation exercise

Here is a relaxation exercise to practise. It will help your mind and body to recover from the impact of stress. It involves tensing muscles and then letting them go. It takes five minutes and can be done at home or in the office.

- In tensing and relaxing your muscles as described below, carry out one stage at a time as automatically as possible without any fuss. Do not anxiously examine a muscle to see if it is relaxed. All you have to do is simply tense and untense your muscles.

- Take off your shoes and loosen any tight clothing. Lie flat on the floor with your head on a pillow or cushion. Make yourself comfortable. Keep your hands at your side. Don't have one leg crossed over the other.

- Now relax your muscles as follows: wrinkle your forehead, then let go. Roll your head around a few times. Clench your teeth together, then let go by letting your lower jaw sag. Tense your neck by drawing your head forward off the cushion, then recline it back to the cushion. Shrug your shoulders towards your ears, then drop them back. Tighten your fists and stiffen your arms, then let go; let your fingers spread out and become loose. Pull your stomach in, then let go. Stiffen your thighs, legs, knees and tense your toes by bringing them upward, then let go.

- Close you eyes and feel a sense of complete calm. Keep on saying to yourself: 'Let go . . . let go . . .' for a minute or so.

- Begin to breathe in and out slowly and deeply through the nose, and be aware of your breath as it enters and leaves your nostrils.

- Say to yourself in this relaxed state, 'I feel very relaxed . . . I feel wonderful. Tension is leaving my body with each outgoing breath. My body is storing up energy. There is nothing else in the world I ought to be doing at this moment. I am capable of achieving anything if I put my mind to it.'

- Relax for a few minutes. You could if you wish tell yourself to go asleep for five minutes and wake up in five minutes time.

- Now gradually bring yourself back to your normal activities.

Management and the life stages

As a manager it is useful for you to be aware of the concept of life stages. Where a person happens to be in his or her life cycle at a particular time affects his or her work performance. The broad categories are as follows:

20s This is the period of career identification. The person begins to climb the ladder in his or her chosen career, gaining experience and, if necessary, taking further courses and examinations.

30s This is a key competitive, energetic and creative period as the person develops his or her track record. It is also a questionning period. Am I in the right career? What can I do to improve my professional development?

40s This is the period of the mid-life crisis. There is an increasing awareness of a time squeeze, the inevitability of death, a lesser time remaining, and the gap between aspirations and achievements. The person is more aware of premature deaths, hospitalization and marriage break-ups. He might ask questions such as: What is this life all about now that I am doing what I am 'supposed' to be doing? Is what I am the only way and the right way? Is there still time to change? Am I too competitive/too ambitious? What are my values? Should I change my job? (Many people change their job for the last time in their forties.) How is my marriage progressing? Do I spend enough time with my spouse and children?

50s Having survived the mid-life crisis there is now an 'acceptance of life' and an increasing dedication to more permanent and central personal values. Life is restructured in terms of time left to live rather than time since birth. A longing for simplicity and the simple life can emerge, an acceptance of what I have and the course I have taken.

Older managers may need reassurance, more frequent and more direct demonstrations that they are held in esteem. Very often they appreciate being given the mentor role of developing younger managers.

60s + The person is coming towards retirement. The secret of retirement is, however, to retire from a career to something else.

Managing your career

Managers who have successful careers always seem to take the right job at the right time. These rules will help you manage your career successfully:

- Know what you want to achieve in your career and what you are prepared to sacrifice in terms of your home, family, interests, etc., to achieve it.

- If appropriate, plan together with your spouse or partner. Set out the career paths to be followed.

- Find a mentor who will guide you through your choices.

- Be an outstanding performer at each stage in your career.

- Don't leave a job because of dissatisfaction with it. Only leave to move into a job which fits into your career path.

- Try to develop a relationship with your boss which will allow you to discuss career options with him or her.

- Avoid dead-end positions which may have short-term advantages, for example, bonuses or travel.

- When leaving a job, leave it in good order with relationships intact.

- Practise self-nomination, let superiors know of your interest in positions.

- Be prepared to take a lateral move to widen your experience.

- Prepare now for your next couple of moves, for instance, learn languages, undertake a course of study.

- Don't keep your light under a bushel; make sure others know of your successes.

- Keep an up-to-date curriculum vitae. Make sure it is produced to the highest quality, fully reflecting your qualifications, experience and achievements.

- Keep expanding your job at each level.

- Don't stay in one job too long.

- Avoid the Peter Principle, being promoted to the level of your incompetence.

Assessing a career move

The following guidelines will help you to assess whether a career move is best for you. There are many factors to be taken into account. Remember that you must not only consider the position itself, but anything which could affect your performance in the new job. Give yourself time to consider a career move, and make sure to discuss it with your spouse and with someone who is familiar with your work.

- Does the career move fit into your long-term career plan?

- Are you moving to a clearly better career position or are you simply leaving your current position for a change?

- Will the new position give you new skills/knowledge?

- Will you be more marketable after moving into the new position?

- What policies apply for training and development in the new position?

- Will you have more work interests and challenges after the newness of the position has worn off?

- Are there opportunities for further career growth and development?

- What are the reporting relationships?

- What is the new job title and how does it compare with the titles of your peers?

- Are there clear job objectives, key result areas and standards of performance set for the new position?

- Is high performance rewarded?

- How do the degrees of control and autonomy compare with your existing position?

- What will your new colleagues and peers be like?

- What are the travel requirements of the position?

- What employee relations practices apply?

- Is your new employer an equal opportunities employer?

- What norms obtain with regard to hours of work?

- What is job security like?

- What salary and fringe benefits apply?

- Does the geographic location suit you and do you have location security?

2 Leadership

It is sometimes difficult to think of yourself as a leader, especially if your work group is small or you are not a senior manager. Leadership is often associated with heroic acts in difficult circumstances. Yet leadership is called for any time your group relies on you to help them achieve their goals. It can take different forms depending on the nature of the group and the environment in which it is operating. This section demonstrates the different styles of leadership, and offers guidance as to the styles you should adopt in a specific situation.

The section includes a guide on the ability to influence the behaviour of others. It identifies a number of different sources of power which you can call on to augment the power given to you as a manager. One important source of power is political action, which is not as sinister as it may sound. It deals with ways in which you can obtain support from other members of the organization for your actions.

Ultimately, your success as a leader depends on your ability to develop your work group so that it becomes an effective team, one in which group members work for each other as well as for themselves. The guides in this section define the characteristics of effective work groups and the steps that have to be followed to develop teamwork. They also deal with the nature and causes of conflict in groups, and how you should manage it.

The guide on staff training and development shows that there are many ways in which you can develop the competence of the team members, particularly by using on-the-job experience.

The manager as leader

In all areas of human endeavour – military, political, sporting – there are great leaders. No fewer examples can be found in organizations, whether commercial, charitable or educational. Yet researchers and academics alike have failed to agree on common core characteristics of effective leaders. Effective leadership in action, however, is easy to identify. In organizational terms, the leader/manager achieves through the action of his or her group. There are three key elements to organizational leadership:

- Identification of workgroup objectives and goals.

- Development of a plan to achieve them.

- Employee commitment to working towards them

The manager as leader, depending on circumstances, is engaged in the following activities:

- Setting objectives and goals.

- Developing a work plan.

- Organizing resources

- Selecting and developing employees.

- Managing employee performance

- Communicating

- Problem solving and decision making

Choosing a leadership style

Which style of leadership should you adopt when you are making a decision? A democratic style, an autocratic style or something in between? Try to match your style to the stage of development of your work group. Consider these factors:

Training and experience
Are they fully trained in all aspects of their work? How much experience have they? How did they respond to difficulties in the past? Have they the skills and knowledge required in the situation?

Ability and resourcefulness
Have you confidence in their managerial and personal characteristics to handle situations? Are they creative in dealing with problems? Do they respond well to crises? Have they the resilience to stay with the task?

Motivation and responsibility
How do they feel about accepting responsibility for decision making? Will they perform better if you give them responsibility? Are they motivated to achieve the required results?

There are five main styles of leadership from which to choose:

- *Tell:* make the decision yourself and simply inform your work group.

- *Sell:* make the decision yourself and sell the decision to your work group.

- *Consultative:* obtain the opinions of your work group before making a decision yourself.

- *Participative:* involve your group in the decision making process

- *Democratic:* leave the decision to your work group.

You should adapt your leadership style to the stage of development of your work group. The more they are trained, capable and motivated, the more democratic your style should become. Your task as a manager is to develop your work group so that you can move with confidence to this more democratic style and so make use of the full potential of the people who work for you.

Power

Power is the ability to influence the behaviour of others. It is an essential characteristic of managerial action. Successful managers achieve through other people – subordinates, colleagues and superiors.

The most obvious source of power is authority. But within an organization there are others, and the effective manager must be able to tap a number of sources.

Legitimate power
As a manager, your position gives you authority over your subordinates. There are other sources of legitimate power. These include 'acceptance', for example, your rank may give you power over other employees not of the same rank when this is accepted in your organization. Legitimate power can also be given to the representative or agent of someone in authority.

Ability to reward
People who can influence the rewards of other employees or who have control over resources have power proportionate to their discretion to apply those rewards or resources.

Ability to coerce
The ability to coerce or to punish others is a source of power. Sometimes this ability is legitimate – for example, a personnel manager under a disciplinary procedure – or it may derive from personal power. An example of the latter would be a dominant personality who has the ability to 'put down' others.

Referent power
Managers who are charismatic or are well liked have an ability to influence others over and above their strict authority. They get this power from colleagues or subordinates wishing to be associated with the actions of such a manager.

Expert power
If the manager is a credible expert in some area, colleagues and subordinates are likely to go along with what he or she says. This is particularly true in a crisis or when an urgent decision has to be made and there is little time for debate.

Information
'Information is power' is a well-known saying. The manager with comprehensive information about a particular situation gains power in much the same way as the credible expert.

Affiliative power
This power comes to managers who affiliate themselves to more powerful people. Some of their power is passed on to the manager who will often be considered to speak on behalf of more powerful associates.

Group power
The power of the group is sometimes greater than the sum of the powers of the individual members of the group, especially where the manager is perceived to be the formal or informal spokesperson for the group.

Political action
Some managers increase their power through 'political' action. They do this by gaining the support of the other managers for their causes.

Organizational politics

Being political is a natural activity for people in organizations. A manager is acting politically when he or she canvasses support for a proposal or takes a position with a view to gaining support from others. In some cases politics can be a positive force within organizations. Its bad name comes from situations in which managers act politically for self-interest or to undermine a legitimate authority within the organization. Effective managers are aware of the political reality of their organizations and can act accordingly to achieve their objectives. Here are some examples of positive political activities:

- Develop relationships with influential people.

- Try to understand the position of objectors.

- Build professional and personal stature.

- Proceed in logical stages keeping others informed of your actions.

- Be prepared to explain your decisions.

- Canvass the support of everyone affected by your decisions.

- Develop strong communication channels.

- Maintain positional flexibility.

- Recognize the assistance of supporters.

- Develop a group of confidants who will give you feedback on yourself and your position.

- Let others speak on your behalf.

- Move rapidly during a crisis.

Effective work groups

One of the ways to increase your effectiveness as a manager is through convincing your subordinates to act as a team. Team building results in synergy so that the output from the team is greater than the total individual contributions. Many groups don't develop into effective teams without deliberate team building activities on the part of the manager. The first step in the process is to identify the characteristics of effective teams:

- *Clear objectives:* the teams knows why it exists and what it is trying to achieve.

- *Well defined key result areas:* team members know what they must do in order to be successful.

- *Agreed standards of performance:* team members agree on the measures of success for each key result area.

- *Clear roles:* each member of the team knows what areas of responsibility he or she is responsible for.

- *Openness and trust:* members feel free to voice their opinions and have confidence in their colleagues.

- *Support and warmth:* team members help each other, are friendly and create a pleasant work environment.

- *Cooperation:* members are flexible and are prepared to help each other.

- *Effective rules and procedures:* the extent of these is in keeping with the nature and purpose of the work group.

- *Sound working practices:* the working practices of the group are reviewed regularly and updated to the best competitive practice.

- *Appropriate leadership:* the manager's leadership style reflects the ability and motivation of the work group.

- *Group processes:* appropriate group processes, for example communications, problem solving and decision making are in place.

- *Measurement systems:* the group members are able to measure their outputs, etc., on an ongoing basis.

- *Feedback systems:* group members get collective and individual feedback on their performance regularly.

- *Constructive conflict:* is encouraged and destructive conflict resolved.

- *Training and development:* the training needs of individual members are assessed and acted on.

- *External relations:* the group develops its relationships with other groups through liaison staff and effective communication processes.

Developing teamwork

A manager cannot rely on teamwork developing automatically without a conscious effort on his or her part. Without the manager's influence teamwork may develop to some extent, but the work group is unlikely to reach full maturity, that is, maximum task performance and member satisfaction.

There are five stages in team development. In the early stages the emphasis is on task issues like work definition, assigning roles, establishing rules and procedures. In the later stages, the emphasis moves towards optimizing group contributions and improving how the members feel about the functioning of the group.

The manager needs to be aware of the stage of development of his or her work group. He or she should try to lead the work group through the different stages. If teamwork problems persist, the manager may have to introduce some teambuilding exercises to improve the effectiveness of the work group.

Forming
During this introductory stage, members try to find out what the nature and the purpose of the group is. How are they supposed to behave? What are the objectives and goals of the group and what part/roles are they supposed to play? Each member is concerned mostly with himself or herself. Politeness disguises the lack of real in-depth communications. Members share little about themselves although they are curious/suspicious about others. The manager/leader makes most decisions for the group.

Storming
Group members react to the nature of the group tasks and to the demands placed on them. Some seek to gain positions of influence. Other members withdraw and/or absent themselves physically or emo-

tionally from the workings of the group. Differences emerge in terms of individual and group commitment, task priority, means and methods as well as who has the expertise. It is a difficult time for the group but must be seen through, otherwise differences will continue to emerge at later stages.

Norming

Now the group is in a position to agree on what has to be done, how it is to be done and what roles the different group members will take. Rules, procedures and processes, for example problem solving and decision making, are settled. Norms of behaviour, accepted ways of acting in the group (some helpful, others not so) develop. There is greater respect for the thoughts and feelings of other group members. A wide range of opinions is accepted and some risky issues can be raised. Some groups never reach this stage and ultimately disintegrate through lack of cohesiveness and effectiveness.

Performing

This stage is the optimum stage of group development. Strong teamwork ensures that group and individual goals are met. The group generates its own energy and the ability of its members is used to the full. There is role and task flexibility and an appropriate style of leadership for a mature group is evident.

Mourning

When the group sees the end approaching, members begin to distance themselves from group processes and activities, resulting in unfinished business, both task and interpersonal. The manager's job is to ensure that the work of the group does not end prematurely, or that members do not believe that it will, Unfinished business should be completed, and the group should be given an opportunity to celebrate its achievements and to disperse in good order.

Conflict between groups

The traditional view of conflict in organizations was that it is unnecessary and harmful. This view no longer prevails. Conflict is seen as inevitable. Absence of it may indicate stagnation or groupthink. Conflict can result from healthy competition. A moderate level of it is essential for optimum performance. The manager's job is to maintain at an acceptable level and to provide means for resolving it when it is causing harm.

There are many types of conflict. An individual may experience conflict within himself or herself, for example between values at work and home. Conflict between individuals may result from personality clashes. However, it is with conflict within and between groups that this guide is concerned.

Sources of conflict
There are many sources of conflict. Clearly, the manager must identify the true source of conflict before dealing with it or helping groups to resolve it.

- *Conflict regarding roles:* usually takes the form of deciding who is responsible for what activities.

- *Interpersonal:* differences between individuals.

- *Task interdependence:* the reliance of one group on another for information, people, support, materials, maintenance, finance, etc.

- *Shared resources:* when two or more groups share the same resources, for example equipment, offices, staff, etc.

- *Different perceptions:* these may occur as a result of different beliefs and values, for example trade union and management.

- *Goal differences:* unresolved goal differences may result in conflict. The goals for quality control may conflict with production goals.

- *Differentiation:* different groups may need to operate in different ways. The approach of a credit department to a customer may be very different from that of a sales team. The timescales of a research unit may differ from those of a production department.

Stages in conflict development

The manager needs to be aware of the different stages in conflict development. Where conflict is unnecessary or harmful, generally it is better to resolve it at the earliest stage.

- *Latent:* the causes of future conflict exist.

- *Perceived:* differences between the groups are evident.

- *Felt:* group members feel the conflict as anger, resentment, anxiety, frustration, etc.

- *Manifest:* the conflict is out in the open and is evident from aggression, lack of cooperation and withdrawals of support.

- *Aftermath:* the conflict has either been suppressed or resolved. Are the causes of the conflict eliminated? How do parties feel? How are they acting towards one another?

Managing conflict

Managing conflict in groups means eliminating conflict which is unnecessary and harmful while stimulating that which is helpful to group processes. The objective is to maximize group performance and member satisfaction. As a manager, be aware of the potential for conflict whenever groups interact, particularly during times of change. Be aware of the lack of energy evident in a group where no conflict exists.

Prevent harmful conflict
- Emphasize work group goals over individual goals.

- Establish clear procedures and rules.

- Develop regular communication channels between groups.

- Establish effective problem solving procedures.

- Avoid win-lose outcomes whereby one group gains at the expense of another.

Reduce conflict
- Remove the cause of the conflict.

- Apply rules and procedures.

- Limit group interaction.

- Involve both groups in joint problem solving exercises.

- Establish a liaison position between groups.

- Rotate members between groups.

- Develop the relationship between the group leaders.

- Reward cooperative performance.

- Use teambuilding exercises such as intergroup training or the development of mirror teams.

Stimulate conflict
- Generate competition between groups.

- Create uncertainty, for example ambiguity re goals and methods.

- Bring in outsiders to challenge group values and norms.

- Change structures, procedures, rewards, etc.

- Appoint leaders who encourage different points of view.

Staff training and development

People learn in many ways. In fact, it is possible to identify four different and complementary ways in which people learn. In planning the development of your staff you will find that some staff have a preference for one way rather than another, and you should take these individual preferences into account. Note that staff development costs more in terms of your time than in financial outlay. However, there are few better ways in which a manager can spend time than in improving the performance of his or her work group.

Learn from experience
- *On the job training:* people learn by doing their jobs, particularly when they are given suitable instruction prior to beginning new tasks.

- *Job rotation:* moving your staff through a variety of different jobs widens their experience, increases their flexibility within your work group and is motivating for staff by increasing the variety of their work.

- *New assignments:* delegating some of your work to your staff develops their capabilities and frees you to do higher value work. Be careful not to dump your unwanted chores on them. Attending committee meetings and drafting reports are easily delegated.

Reflect on experience
It has been said that ten years' experience can often be no more than one year's experiences repeated ten times. The value of job experience is greatly enhanced when employees reflect on the experience to consider what worked well and what can be improved.

- *Performance feedback:* don't wait for the annual performance review to discuss employee performance. At least once a quarter, and more often when they are carrying out new tasks, sit down formally with each of your subordinates and discuss how each is getting on with his or her job.

- *Coaching:* in coaching you give individual attention to employees. The process involves setting specific tasks, monitoring performance and reviewing progress on the tasks. When developing employees for future assignments it is useful to include tasks which will be part of their future work. Coaching is also used in skills training sessions during off the job courses.

- *Counselling:* in counselling, subordinates are encouraged to find their own solutions to work problems through a process of guided discussion. It is particularly appropriate in situations where there is no one right answer. It is frequently used for problems involving interpersonal relations.

General principles
- *Off the job training:* these include general management courses as well as courses in specific functional areas. They range from one day awareness courses to four year degree programmes. They are most valuable in preparing subordinates for future positions and for developing new skills and knowledge.

- *Reading:* subordinates should take some responsibility for developing themselves. Managers should facilitate subordinates who do so by making suitable materials, journals, magazines, books, videos, etc., available to them.

- *Professional associations:* membership of these associations and participation in their activities should be encouraged as a means of professional development.

Experimentation
- *Trial and error:* employees should be given the opportunity to try out new ideas. Learning comes from failure as well as from success.

- *Task forces:* membership of task forces and other groups charged with overcoming problems or introducing new ideas can be an invaluable learning experience for subordinates.

• *Pilot programmes:* encourage subordinates to try out their new ideas in pilot programmes designed to test their effect and to establish an accurate measure of the benefits and costs of the new approach.

3 Planning

Many organizations and managers dislike making plans. They see themselves as too action-orientated to waste time drawing up plans. They want to get on with the job. Some managers have had a bad experience of planning. The planning process took too long or the plans themselves were too cumbersome or impractical. On the other hand, there is no surer way to achieve your goals than to have a good plan and to implement it effectively.

By following the guides in this section, you will be able to draw up effective plans, straightforward and flexible, which will have the support of the people you want to implement them. You will also be able to manage the change processes which many plans call for. You will understand the reasons why people resist change and the means by which such resistance can be avoided.

Planning does not have to be a dirty word in your team. It is better to take a long time with planning at the expense of implementation than the other way around. The first step is to be aware of the barriers to planning and to learn how to avoid them. The next step is to draw up your plans in a way which ensures that they are practical and well supported, and how they can be successfully implemented.

A technique known as 'critical path analysis' will enable you to schedule a complex series of activities in the most efficient way.

Pressures from outside and inside your organization will require you to manage change within your work group. Technological and systems change are the norm nowadays, but you may also have to change the behaviours or even the beliefs and values of members of your team. Such changes will frequently be resisted. An effective plan will incorporate a change management strategy to help you avoid resistance to change. Forcefield analysis is a valuable technique to help you prepare your strategy.

Making plans

Planning is the process by which human, technological, administrative and financial activities are directed towards achieving organizational objectives. When circumstances change, the manager must plan to meet the requirements of the new situation. In making a plan, the manager predetermines how he or she will use the resources available. Planning determines what is to be done, how it is to be done, when it is to be done and by whom. It is an integral part of every manager's job.

Types of plan
There are three main types of plan:

- *Strategic plan:* this is the plan which determines what business the organization is in, its mission, objectives and goals, together with the strategy for competing effectively. It has three key characteristics: it embraces all the activities of the organization, has a long time horizon (three to ten years), and its successful implementation is critical for the organization's success. It is formulated by the top management team.

- *Operational plans:* these are the plans developed by the individual units within an organization to give effect to the strategic plan. Most managers are required from time to time to develop operational plans. They should take the initiative in developing work plans for their own areas on an annual basis, and other plans as the need arises.

- *Standing plans:* these plans cover the routine activities of the organization and include the organization's policies, procedures and rules.

The elements of a plan

A good plan details what is to be done, how and by when. It includes the following elements:

- *Clear objective and goals:* the objective is a general statement of the purpose of the plan, for example to increase sales of product X. Goals are specific measures of performance, for instance to increase sales of product X in a certain region to a given amount by a certain date.

- *Present position:* the plan should include a statement of the present position. It should detail the reasons why the objective and goals have been set, the resources currently available and the difficulties to be faced in implementation.

- *Resources required:* this part of the plan sets out the human, technological, administrative and financial resources required to achieve the objective and goals.

- *Work programme:* the programme sets out the main activities which must be completed if the plan is to succeed. It will identify priority actions, the order in which activities will take place and who is responsible for taking action.

- *Schedule:* the schedule sets out the dates and timing of the various activities. It will highlight activities which must be completed before other activities. Various techniques such as critical path analysis are available to managers responsible for complex scheduling.

- *Control mechanisms:* the plan should incorporate control mechanisms by which progress against the plan can be measured by management. These are crucial in complex or long term plans. Milestones, which determine how much work should be completed by a certain date, are useful control mechanisms.

- *Contingency plans:* an organization's plans should include contingency plans to be put into effect in the event of significant change in circumstances.

- *Statement of assumptions:* a plan which is critical to the success of an organization should set out the assumptions upon which it is based with perhaps a statement of the probability of the assumptions being correct.

Barriers to planning

Many managers prefer to start on the implementation of activities rather than take the time to develop a plan. There are many reasons why thls is so. Yet the Japanese have repeatedly demonstrated that time spent planning is more than made up through speedy and successful implementation. The manager must plan to overcome the barriers to planning.

Barriers to planning

- *Organizational:* some organizations do not favour a formal planning approach. The reasons are many. Sometimes the pace of change is so fast that there is a feeling that plans will become obsolete before they have been fully implemented. Another organizational problem is a belief that planning is an academic activity and that managers should get 'stuck in'.

- *Individual:* many managers avoid planning because they do not want to commit themselves to objectives, goals and timescales. They may be unwilling to give up their own pet projects in favour of the planned activities. Some managers have a fear of failure and believe that a plan may commit them to a level of performance which they may be unable to attain or sustain. They may not wish to risk their self-esteem or their job security on the success of a plan. Another factor is that reward systems within organizations do not always encourage managers to embark on major plans. There may be no benefits for succeeding although there are penalties for failure.

- *Time and expense:* the best plans are made by involving some or all of the people who will be required to implement them. Planning can be a time consuming and expensive process. The argument is that it is better to get started and get the job done rather than spend time developing plans.

Overcome barriers to planning

- *Making time for planning:* planning is part of a manager's job. Time must be found for it in the same way as for other aspects of managerial work.

- *Make planning a routine:* prepare plans as a matter of routine and encourage subordinates to do likewise. Keep the format and the style of plans simple.

- *Involve subordinates:* much of the fear of the planning process can be overcome by involving subordinates in the plan from its earliest stages of development. Involvement of subordinates will also result in a high level of commitment to the plan.

- *Review plans regularly:* keep the schedule of the activities visible for all to see. Pin the schedule on a notice board and conduct regular reviews modifying the plan to meet changing circumstances.

- *Closure:* when the plan has been successfully completed notify everyone who was involved, and if possible celebrate the completion in some suitable way.

Making plans effective

A frequent criticism of plans is that they are impractical. The following steps will ensure that the plans you make are practical and well supported and can be successfully implemented.

- Your work unit plans should support and be compatible with the stategic business plan and the operational plans of the work group.

- Before preparing a plan, discuss its objectives and goals with your superior and ask him or her to obtain top management support.

- Keep the planning process as simple as possible, and avoid the temptation to develop paper mountains.

- The plan you introduce should follow established practices within your organization. The more your plan deviates from established practices, the greater the implementation problems you will experience. Avoid unnecessary changes, but do not be afraid to establish challenging objectives and goals.

- Use participative approaches in developing your plan. Involve, at an early stage, everyone who will be affected, including those responsible for implementation, those who will benefit and those who must supply resources, for example other departments, customers, etc.

- Communicate to subordinates and to others why specific actions are to be taken.

- Check that the resources necessary are available before you start.

- Sell the benefits of the plan regularly throughout its period of implementation.

- Keep the plan flexible so that it can adjust to changing circumstances.

- Build in milestones and provide for the regular review of progress.

Critical path analysis

Critical path analysis is a very useful technique for ensuring that a plan is completed on time. It helps you when you have to schedule a large number of activities. When preparing a plan, you will find that some activities must be completed before others (in series). Other activities can be completed simultaneously (in parallel). Critical path analysis tells you the shortest time in which all the activities can be completed. It highlights those for which timing is critical and on which you must concentrate attention and resources.

For complex activities there are very good computer programs which are user friendly and can be learned within one hour. Most plans can be completed manually.

- List all the activities with their earliest start dates and their duration in days/weeks. What activities can be done in parallel? What activities must be done in series? Where resources permit, it is desirable to carry out activities in parallel rather than in series.

- Prepare a piece of graph paper by marking the days/weeks through to the completion of the project.

- Plot the activities on the graph paper. The critical path is the sequence of in series activities which requires the longest time for completion. Follow the example in Figure 3.1.

- So far as possible, schedule parallel activities in a way that reduces demand on resources required by the critical path activities.

- Be sure to allow time for hold-ups, maintenance and late deliveries. Some activities on the critical path can be done in a different way so as to reduce the duration of the total activities.

- Distribute copies of the critical path analysis to everyone involved

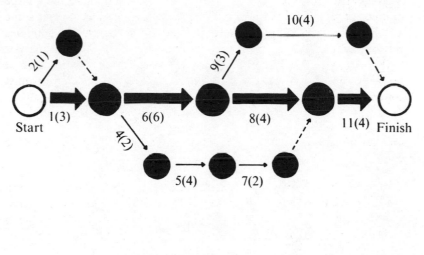

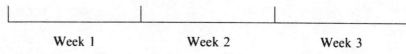

Figure 3.1
Critical path diagram. ——▶: Activities, ●: completion of activities, ( ): time taken by activity in days,‒ ‒ ‒ ‒ : dummy activity to complete diagram, ⟹ : critical path. Activities 1–6–8–11 are on the critical path. Total time for project: 17 days.

in implementing the plan so that they understand the importance of completing activities on time.

- Control the process by monitoring progress against the schedule. Generally, a slippage in activities which are not on the critical path does not affect the total timing. Delay in the critical activities requires immediate action to speed up some other activity on the critical path. Otherwise the plan will not be implemented on time

Managing change

A manager must be sure that work is done both efficiently and effectively. Efficiency comes from establishing work practices, administrative systems, procedures and rules. Effectiveness comes from changing the work in response to changing demands from outside and inside the organization. Managing change is difficult because it involves undoing many past actions and practices. Resistance to change on the part of members of the work group, is common at all levels in an organization. Pressure for change comes from both outside and inside the organization.

External forces

- *Economic:* changes in interest rates, currency exchange rates, inflation and consumer demand.

- *Legal:* product liability, employment law, commercial regulations.

- *Technology:* automation, computerized systems and transport.

- *Competition:* entry of new competitors or existing competitors changing strategies.

- *Social:* demographic changes, changes in lifestyles, changes in beliefs and values of people.

- *Political:* protectionism, free trade, political upheaval.

Internal

- *Products:* introduction of new products and services.

- *Technology:* changes in processes and machinery.

- *Structure:* changes in organizational structure, for instance divisionalization, changes in policies and procedures.

- *Social:* changes in beliefs and values of employees, changes in leadership in the organization, etc.

Types of change

Managers must be able to adapt their work units to four major types of change. It is unusual, nowadays, to make one type of change without making others. Generally speaking, changes to subordinates' beliefs and values are the most difficult to introduce.

- *Technological:* automation, computerization, new machinery.

- *Systems:* new administrative and work systems, rules and procedures.

- *Behaviours:* new work practices and changes in work habits, for example shift working, overtime arrangements, holiday schedules, tea breaks, etc.

- *Beliefs and values:* the other three types of changes affect what people do. This type seeks to change the way people think, for instance about their work, management, colleagues, unions

Four step process

Managing change is a four step process.

- Create dissatisfaction with the current situation. Point out the flaws and faults in the current way of doing things. Better still, encourage your work group to find the flaws themselves.

- Create a vision of a desired future state. Show how things would be better if changes were introduced. Demonstrate how people can benefit from the changes.

- Prepare a plan setting out practical steps to introduce the change. Involve your work group in the process. Try to reduce fear of the change. Plan how you will manage the transition state between the old and the new.

- Consolidate your change. Develop new systems, work practices and procedures to prevent a slippage back to the old way of doing things.

Overcoming resistance to change

Most managers find that no matter what change they try to introduce, they experience resistance. To overcome resistance identify its cause. Develop a strategy for dealing with it. Remember also that different employees have different reasons why they prefer the status quo.

- *Self-interest:* employees may suffer an economic loss by virtue of change, for example loss of overtime earnings. They may also suffer a loss of status, privileges or self esteem, for instance craft workers when new technology is introduced.

- *Fear of unknown:* employees may be uncertain about how they will adapt to the changed situation. Will they have the aptitudes, knowledge and skills required? This fear frequently arises when new technology is being introduced.

- *Conscientious objection:* well informed employees may have a genuine, sincerely held, if mistaken, belief that the change is wrong. Changes are easier to introduce if everyone feels that the proposed change is correct.

- *Lack of trust:* employees may doubt the motives of managers whom they do not trust, for example they may refuse to accept assurances of job security when new machinery is being introduced.

- *Different perceptions:* no two people see things in exactly the same way. An accountant may see a problem in financial terms when an engineer sees it in a technical terms.

- *Lack of tolerance:* some employees have no tolerance for change. They want things to remain just as they are and do not want the inconvenience of adapting to change. They may be cynical about past changes.

- *Cultural:* employees may refuse to accept change because it conflicts with their beliefs and values. They believe that what has been good for them in the past should not be given up easily. For this reason unionized employees are often reluctant to accept changes to manning levels, demarcation and restrictive practices. Senior employees also experience difficulty in adapting, for example to open plan offices, or to the emergence of single status conditions of employment.

Change strategies
Identify the cause of the resistance to change, then select the most appropriate strategy for overcoming it. There is a wide range of strategies. Sometimes a number must be used in combination.

- *Persuasion:* present logical and emotional arguments to subordinates.

- *Participation:* involves subordinates in the identification of a need for change and the selection of the appropriate change.

- *Facilitation:* help employees to cope with the change, for instance use a transition period to give employees time to adapt to the change or arrange transfers/early retirements for employees who can't.

- *Education:* educate employees with regard to the need for and consequences of change; for instance, arrange a visit to a location where the change is operating. Train employees in the skills and knowledge needed to adapt to the changed situation.

- *Individual cases:* sometimes the general acceptance by the work group for a change is withheld until individual cases are dealt with, and your strategy should focus on addressing the needs of those individuals.

- *Negotiation:* a bargaining process whereby you offer additional benefits to employees who agree to the change. Do not compromise the benefits of the change in these negotiations or dilute the effectiveness of the change.

- *Coercion:* forcing subordinates to accept the change. You must have the power to force them to comply. It is a strategy of last resort and should only be used when other approaches have failed. Coercion should be used in combination with education and facilitation to bring about acceptance of the change at a future time.

74

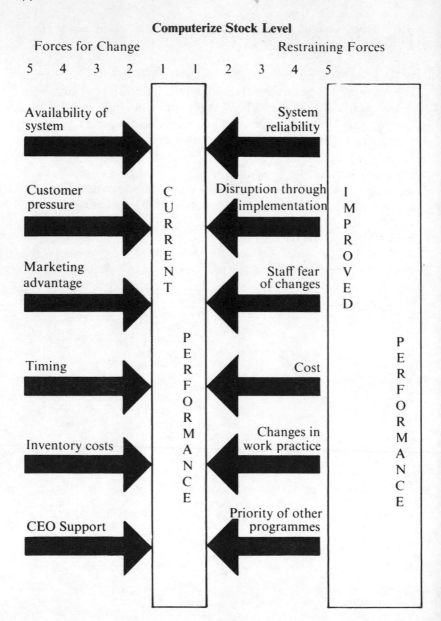

Figure 3.2
Forcefield diagram (1–5 indicates strength of force)

Forcefield analysis

Forcefield analysis can be a valuable aid to managers planning a change programme. It helps them to develop a vision of all the forces acting for and against the change. It is based on Kurt Lewin's theory that the current way you do things is the result of a balance between driving and restraining forces. If you wish to introduce a change you have to change the balance of forces either by increasing the driving force for change or reducing the restraining forces. Generally speaking, it is more efficient to reduce the restraining forces because sometimes increasing the driving forces may also increase the restraining forces. For example, if you wish to increase the output of your work group you may try to push them harder. This approach may give rise to resentment and dissatisfaction on the part of the work group, resulting in lower output.

Another advantage of forcefield analysis is that it reduces the tendency to look for simplistic solutions such as putting down resistance to change to a single cause.

The steps in setting up a forcefield analysis are as follows:

- List all the forces for and against the change.

- Assign a strength to each force on a 1 – 5 scale (5 being the highest force).

- Set out the forces in a diagram, like that in Figure 3.2.

- Consider strategies to reduce the forces against change.

- Consider actions to enhance the forces in favour of change

- Assess the feasibility and priority of each action.

- Develop a plan to implement the actions.

4 Recruitment and Selection

Most managers are not involved very often in recruitment and selection decisions. Two or three times a year is the norm. For that reason, many of them have little opportunity to develop their skills in this area. The result is mediocre or bad decisions with which they have to live for a long time. Very often the decision is based on the establishment of a good rapport with one candidate. This intuitive reaction is a legitimate element in the process, but it is not a substitute for a systematic approach.

Once a vacancy has been defined, the first step is job design. By considering the basics you ensure that the person you select will make the maximum contribution to your work group. The job design process will result in a job description. This outlines the job purpose and the principal responsibilities of the position, together with some of the critical dimensions of the job, such as work relationships and authority. Only when you have a completed job description can you decide on the person specification, that is, the characteristics of the person you want to fill the job.

You can ensure a good choice of suitable applicants by preparing an effective job advertisement to attract the right sort of candidates. Once you have done this you can start planning the selection process. Most managers rely heavily on the selection interview to decide who will be offered the job. However, there are a number of points which must be considered before the interview process starts. The most important of these is to determine the criteria for success in the job, and to establish the way in which all candidates will be assessed equally against these criteria.

Badly conducted interviews lead to poor selection decisions. The guides in this section will help you to improve your interviewing techniques. They help you plan the interview and choose questions which give you useful information for the selection decision.

Other guides deal with finalizing the recruitment process. The most important of these include checking references, making the job offer and giving feedback to unsuccessful candidates.

Job design

Job design is the process of achieving optimum fit between people and jobs, either by designing new jobs or by redesigning old ones. It is always a good idea to review the distribution of responsibilities in your work group whenever a vacancy arises. There are significant advantages to involving your staff in the process. Be prepared to be radical in your approach. However, there is no one best way, and there are advantages and disadvantages to the various approaches you can take. The issues relating to job design apply equally, when considering the total tasks of a work group, as well as those of an individual employee.

There are five key factors to consider when designing a job:

- The range of skills required to complete the tasks.

- The degree of autonomy you can give the job holder.

- The extent to which the job holder completes a discrete piece of work.

- The significance of the task, in terms of its impact on others and on the organization.

- The amount and timing of feedback given to the job holder.

There are three main approaches to job design:

- *Specialization:* increases efficiency by facilitating recruitment and training for routine or specialized work; by enabling employees to become expert in their work; it may result in a decrease in job satisfaction due to boredom or frustration.

- *Job enlargement:* increases the variety of tasks or functions performed by the job holder, through combining two or more jobs into one, or by rotating employees through a number of jobs.

- *Job enrichment:* increases the job satisfaction of job holders by giving them more control, the way the work is done and by making them responsible for results.

The following procedure will help you in the process of job design:

- List of all the activities of the work group.

- Group them into natural and logical work clusters.

- Eliminate redundant tasks or duplications.

- Combine two or more jobs into one or take a number of tasks/functions and put them into a single job. This is job enlargement.

- Give the job holders greater responsibility to set their own pace, decide on work methods, solve their own problems, control their own costs. This is job enrichment.

- Build in feedback systems so that employees know how well they are performing.

- Involve employees in the process. Ask them if they were given a free hand to design their own jobs, what changes they would make.

- So far as possible, ensure that employees are satisfied with the results.

Job descriptions

A job description describes the purpose, scope, responsibilities, tasks and relationships which form a particular job. The personnel department is usually involved in helping line management to draw up job descriptions based on evidence from:

- the immediate supervisor/manager.

- the person actually doing the job.

- training documents, which may reveal aspects of the job neglected in practice.

The employee's manager may be asked to list his or her expectations of the subordinate whilst the subordinate lists the tasks he or she actually does. The new job description marries the two lists.

The final job description contains:

- the job title.

- job relationships including superior(s) and subordinates.

- the purpose of the job.

- the main duties/responsibilities.

- authority to approve, for example expenditure, disciplinary action.

- any other conditions applying specifically to the job, for instance travel, location, hours of work.

Job descriptions are used primarily to define an employee's job responsibilities and to determine the division of duties between employees. They are also used for job evaluation exercises and for purposes of performance appraisal.

The person specification

Once you have a clear idea from the job description of the work to be done, you can focus on the kind of person you are looking for to carry out this job effectively. What essential qualities, abilities, knowledge, motivation, etc., must he or she have? You can use the following questions to help you draw up a profile of the person. Distinguish between essential and desirable characteristics.

- What educational standards are required?

- Are professional qualifications essential? Are licences needed to do the work?

- What experience is required? Describe it in terms of years doing certain kinds of work – managerial, technical and administrative.

- Any special attitudes required, for example manual dexterity, languages/verbal or numerical skills, etc.

- What personal characteristics are appropriate? Physical characteristics include appearance, height, weight, voice and health. Personality characteristics include leadership skills, maturity, dedication, creativity, etc.

- Any special circumstances required, for instance prepared to travel, health, etc.?

- Care should be taken not to include unnecessary restrictions relating to sex, age, etc., which in many countries are in any case illegal.

Before the interview

It is important to prepare well to ensure that you select the right person for the job. Use this procedure.

- Draw up a job description and a person specification.

- Decide whether to advertise.

- Decide the correct grade and salary range for the job. What salary can you offer?

- Decide what tests (if appropriate) to administer. They may include psychometric tests, structured interviews, etc.

- Decide carefully whether to interview alone or to have a panel interview. Having experienced selectors present at the interview may lead to a more objective assessment of the candidates than if you interview alone. However, more than two interviewers at a time may stop you establishing rapport with the interviewee.

- Ensure that the physical setting is private and comfortable and likely to create a good impression of your unit.

- Decide in advance how to determine whether a candidate meets the requirements of the person specification; for example, are you looking for formal qualifications, work experience or both?

- Most importantly, decide what skills and knowledge are required, and how you will determine whether the candidates are qualified.

- List the selection criteria and make sure you assess all candidates against the same criteria. Ideally, all the candidates should be assessed in precisely the same way.

Recruitment advertising

Effective advertising helps to attract the right candidates to apply for a position. The advertising can be both internal and external. Before going outside your organization it can be more economical and morale boosting to see whether there is anyone already on the payroll who could do the job. Compose an advertisement designed to attract the greatest number of applications, and use selection methods to identify the best candidate.

Here are the main steps in recruitment advertising:

- Finalize time scale/degree of urgency for the recruitment process and decide the budget available for advertising.

- Consider the various sources for recruitment – external/internal as appropriate. External includes employment agencies, professional bodies, poaching, press/radio/TV advertising, job centres, educational establishments, personal contact. Internal includes noticeboards, newsletters, house magazines, employees' pay envelopes.

- The advertisement should include the job title, a job summary, a broad description of the ideal candidate, salary (specified or negotiable), grade (if the advert is internal), working conditions, to whom the person reports and how to respond to the advert.

- Mention job enhancing factors such as: the prestige of the company; the work is interesting; it offers advancement; the company's education and training policy; fringe benefits; holiday entitlements; sports and social facilities; opportunities for travel, etc.

- Ensure that the copy is legal (avoiding sexual and other forms of discrimination).

During the interview

An effective interview is a conversation with a purpose, namely, to find the right person for the job, the person with the right attitude and aptitudes to fill the vacancy. The effective interview also ensures that candidates receive sufficient information on which to base their own impressions about the company and job. Your objective during an interview is to get the candidate to do most of the talking. The following approach will help you to conduct a smooth and successful interview.

- Welcome and relax the candidate (smile). Introduce yourself and your role. Talk about the company and the job. Outline the interview procedure.

- When the candidate is talking give him or her your complete attention and observe any non-verbal signals. These can often reveal a lot about the candidate. Use silence constructively to keep the candidate talking. This means waiting out short pauses. You may also need to summarize occasionally what the candidate is saying in order to make sure you have properly understand his or her responses.

- Ask open and probing questions. Avoid multiple, loaded and trick questions. Make sure that you ask only one question at a time.

- Encourage openness by the interviewee by praising accomplishments. Do not criticize or indicate disapproval.

- Make notes during the interview, for memory purposes.

- The candidate should do between 70 and 80 per cent of the talking. Your task is to guide the discussion so that it covers the key topics.

- Finally, invite questions from the candidate about the job, summarize the interview and explain the next step. Always end on a positive note.

The seven-point interview plan

Many interviewers use this seven-point plan as a guide to planning an interview.

- *Appearance*
  This area includes factors such as physical appearance, dress, speech and manner.

- *Attainment*
  Included in this area are educational and work achievements.

- *General intelligence*
  Where academic qualifications are insufficient to indicate general intelligence, the interviewer may look for evidence of intelligence outside of the educational system.

- *Special aptitudes*
  Here the interviewer will be investigating whether the job candidate has the skills and aptitudes required to do the job, such as manual dexterity, numerical skills, languages, leadership ability. What other aptitudes, not immediately required, does the candidate have?

- *Interests*
  How does the candidate spend his or her free time? Captaining a football team may indicate leadership ability. A stamp collector may be a loner. However, be careful not to over-emphasize single sources of information. What career interests does the job candidate have?

- *Disposition*
  This area covers the candidate's social personality. Is his or her personality suited to the work? Would he or she fit into your team? Could you have a good relationship with him or her? How would he or she get on with other members of your work group?

- *Circumstances*
  This is a catch-all heading. It includes such factors as health, preparedness to travel, interest in the job, re-location, domestic situation, job expectations and salary requirements.

Types of question and their use

Different types of question should be used at different stages in the interview. Early on ask 'open' questions to encourage the candidate to talk and to build rapport. Open questions can also be used to probe for additional information. Closed and leading questions are used to confirm answers and remove abiguity.

- *Open questions*
  These are used to explore opinions/attitudes and to encourage the person to keep on talking. They usually start with: Who? Why? What? When? Where? How? For example, 'What are your thoughts on . . .?'; 'How did you . . .?'; 'How would you . . .?'; 'Will you tell me about . . .?'.

- *Closed questions*
  Closed questions expect a 'yes'/'no' response. They are used to establish specific facts and information; 'Did you like working for XYZ Co.?' They can also be used to force an unambiguous response from the candidate.

- *Leading questions*
  These questions suggest the answer which is required; 'So you left the job because you did not get on with your boss?'. They are generally considered as bad practice for interviewers even when they are not trick questions.

- *Probing questions*
  These are used to increase the 'depth' of the interview. They encourage the candidate to give more detailed information or explanations. They take many forms and are an essential part of the skilled interviewer's repertoire:

- The straight question, 'Can you elaborate on why you felt unhappy about.?'

- The pause, let the candidate break the silence by elaborating.

- Reflection, 'so you were unhappy about . . .'

- Key word repetition, 'unhappy?'.

- Minimum verbal response . . . 'mmh' or 'yes'.

- Gestures . . . nodding your head to encourage the candidate to continue talking.

- *Summary questions*
  These are used to check understanding. They also confirm your interest and understanding to the candidate; 'So what you are saying is . . .'.

Useful interview questions

Here are some job interview questions. Select the ones most appropriate to the interview you are about to conduct. The questions are not listed in any order of priority. They are all designed to encourage candidates to talk.

- Tell me about yourself.

- Why should we offer you the job?

- What are your strengths for the job?

- What has been your most valuable work experience?

- How would you describe yourself?

- What is your proudest achievement?

- What would you like to be doing in five years' time?

- How ambitious are you?

- How well do you like your current job/company?

- What are some of the things you find less satisfying?

- Why do you think you would be capable of supervising/managing people?

- Have you innovated in your previous/present job? In what way?

- Why do you want this job?

- Why do you think you're suitable for this job?

- What was it about ... that interested you? (for example, technology, personnel).

- Why did you leave that job?

- How do you react to pressure? Give examples.

- What do you think distinguishes a good manager from a bad one?

- What have been the milestones in your career?

- What would you do if ... (some problem related to the job on offer)?

- Why did you move from ... to ...?

- What are your hobbies?

- What experience do you have which is most relevant to the job on offer?

- In what ways have you been able to stamp your own personality on the jobs you've had?

After the interview

Immediately after an interview it is advisable to make a few notes about each candidate whilst your memory is still fresh. It is difficult to remember 'all' about an individual candidate after you have seen many unless you write down your impressions. Here are some general questions you might ask yourself.

- To what extent does the candidate have the essential characteristics set out in the person specification?

- What difficulties have been identified – for example, not prepared to travel, frequency of job changes, unexplained gaps in CV?

- Does the candidate have any of the desirable characteristics?

- How well will the candidate fit into your work group?

- Can you meet the candidate's expectations regarding job title, responsibilities, salary, benefits, etc.?

- If clearly unsuitable, note this on the application form and the person will later be sent a letter of rejection. If there is a doubt you should note this and possibly ask the person back for a second interview along with other short-listed candidates.

Final selection and job offer

Having interviewed all the invited candidates at least once, you are now ready to make the final selection and to offer the job to the successful candidate.

- Before offering the job to the successful candidate, follow up on the references supplied. Normally you should have at least one reference in your possession by the time you conduct the final interview. Always ask the candidate's permission to seek references. It is good practice to follow up on written references with an informal discussion on the 'phone.

- After offering the job (usually over the 'phone) follow up the offer with a letter/contract of employment.

- Complete the records of the interview process and open a file on the new employee.

- Write and thank the unsuccessful candidates.

- Draw up an induction/training programme.

Checking references

Checking references is a very important part of the recruitment process. It is much neglected and often left to juniors in the office. It is your opportunity to get good quality additional information from past colleagues of the job candidate. Non-work references are generally of little value. Many candidates supply written references but the most valuable references are obtained through telephone discussion. Prepare a check list of items you wish to discuss with the referee in advance of the 'phone call. Remember that it is important that you establish an open and trusting relationship with the person giving the reference.

- Give your name, job title and company.

- State the purpose of your call.

- Invite the referee to ring you back at a time convenient for him or her.

- Point out that anything which is said will be kept in strict confidence.

- Ask the referee how long he or she has known the applicant. What was their relationship?

- Use an open question to get a general summary of the candidate's career history with the referee's company.

- Cover specific areas like length of time in each job, how the person related to colleagues, what were the employee's strengths and accomplishments.

- Had the employee any shortcomings? Be specific about any concerns you have.

- Ask open, non-leading questions about why the employee left or intends to leave the job? Ask whether the employee would be rehired in the same or another position.

- End the discussion by asking whether there is anything else the referee would like to say. Thank the referee and confirm again the confidentiality of the discussion.

Giving feedback to non-successful candidates

Very often when there are internal candidates for a position, some of whom may report to you, you may be required to give feedback to a non-successful job candidate. Normally, you would have two objectives for the discussion. Firstly, you will wish to explain the basis of the selection decision. Secondly, you will wish to help the candidate to overcome any loss in self-esteem and to be better positioned for future vacancies. This discussion takes place after the successful candidate has accepted the position.

- Prepare for the discussion by reviewing the extent to which the job candidate met the selection criteria. Decide whether the candidate did not get the job because he or she did not reach the selection criteria or because there was a better qualified candidate.

- Select a suitable time and place for the discussion. Put the candidate at ease. Describe the selection criteria. Explain where the candidate did not meet the selection criteria or how another candidate was more qualified. Encourage questions or comments from the employee.

- If appropriate, suggest that the employee participates in a career counselling interview. Thank the employee for participating. End the discussion in a friendly manner.

- Do not become involved in a detailed discussion regarding other applicants for the position, including the successful one.

5 Managing Employee Performance

There is one common characteristic of successful managers. They make a distinctive impression on the part of the organization for which they are responsible. They identify some particular issues and concerns, for example quality, productivity, creativity, cost, etc. Then, they manage their teams so that members achieve their full potential while emphasizing the same issues and concerns. The result is a high-performing team whose effort is focused on important organizational goals.

The approach taken in the guides in this section is known as 'behaviour modification'. It maintains that people's behaviour is shaped by learning what actions on their part pay off. The manager's ability to influence the recognition and reward of employee performance puts him or her in a powerful position to shape employee behaviour. That is, the manager can direct the effort of his or her team onto key issues and concerns. He or she may use the organization's formal recognition and rewards systems. However, there are also many informal approaches available.

The most important form of recognition and reward available to a manager is verbal feedback, especially positive feedback. It should not be stored up for a holiday but should be given regularly. The annual performance review should simply reflect what has been discussed throughout the year. It does not work in the absence of regular feedback from their manager.

Managing employee performance involves more than behaviour modification, of course. The guides in this section also deal with inducting new employees and giving them training instructions. Effective delegation is important for your own development as well as for that of your subordinates.

The guides on coaching and career counselling emphasize that the manager must demonstrate a genuine concern for the team members as well as for the job they do.

Inducting new employees

This meeting should take place as soon as the new employee reports to work for you, whether from another part of your company or as a new recruit. Review his or her personal file. There should also be office space, a desk, a phone, stationery, etc., made available. Does the new employee need identity badges, parking sticker, etc.?

Allow plenty of time for this meeting. The relationship you develop now will have a long lasting effect.

- Welcome the new employee. Say now pleased you are to have him or her working for you. Engage in a social conversation.

- Describe the objectives and goals of your work unit and how they fit into the total organization's objectives and goals. Review the organizational structure and show how the new employee fits in.

- Review the employee's position objectives, key result areas and goals. Discuss with the employee how to get started, what he or she should be doing during the first weeks on the job. Discuss what resources and facilities are available to the employee, such as secretarial assistance, computer links and reports.

- Plan other induction activities, such as meeting other managers, other team members and specialist training.

- Show the employee his or her office.

- Introduce the employee to colleagues.

- Encourage the employee to ask questions.

- Agree to meet again with the employee at a specific time/date to follow up on the induction process.

Giving training instruction

The following are the usual steps involved in giving training instruction:

- Set the objectives of the instruction, what the trainee will be able to do and to what standard when the training is complete.

- Choose the training method.

- Explain to the trainee what has to be done, including the standards to be achieved and the benefits of achieving them. Give the trainee confidence in his or her ability to succeed.

- Show the trainee what to do: first of all, give an overview of the complete task and then the first stage which the trainee has to master.

- Demonstrate completion of the first task.

- Supervise the trainee at each stage in turn until the appropriate standard is reached.

- Increase the standard required.

- Praise the trainee when something is done well. Point out any problems, but show the solutions as well.

- Evaluate the training from time to time to see if the method or procedure can be improved

Defining performance requirements

Develop performance requirements for your subordinates. Each subordinate needs to know the reasons why his or her job exists, what you consider to be the most important areas of the job, and what standard of performance is required in each of the key areas. Take the time to meet each subordinate individually. Because performance requirements change over time you should have these meetings on a regular basis, at least once a year, and informal reviews quarterly. Research indicates that these meetings are most effective when they are conducted in an open and supportive atmosphere, and the subordinate is given an opportunity to agree the standards of performance.

Accordingly, to define performance requirements with your subordinates, you must discuss job objectives, key result areas and standards of performance.

Job objectives
A job exists to achieve some organizational objective, occasionally a single objective, more often two or three. Job objectives define why the job exists. The job may change, however, from time to time, and it is useful to review objectives on a regular basis. Here are a few examples: a district sales manager might have a single objective to promote sales in a given product range. A safety manager might have two objectives, such as an objective relating to the safety of employees in the factory and a second objective relating to environmental protection.

Key result areas
The next step is to establish those areas in which the subordinate is expected to act. These are known as key result areas, and they are most important part of the subordinate's job. Generally speaking, a subordi-

nate should have no more than eight key result areas. Examples for a district sales manager are:

(a) Staff selection, training and supervision.
(b) Liaising with key customers.
(c) New product introduction and promotion.
(d) Achieving sales targets.
(e) Elimination of discounts.
(f) Reduction in expenses of the sales team.

Standards of performance
The subordinate now knows what he or she is supposed to be doing. The next step is to establish standards of performance which allow you and the subordinate to plan and later evaluate his or her performance. The agreed standards of performance are goals for the employee. To be effective goals should have the following characteristics, which produce the acronym SMART:

- *Specific:* the subordinate should be able to understand what is expected.

- *Measurable:* goals should be quantifiable and the employee should be able to assess on an ongoing basis how he or she is performing against the goals.

- *Attainable but challenging:* the goals should present a challenge to the employee, motivating him or her to higher levels of performance.

- *Relevant:* goals should be related to one of the key result areas.

- *Time-orientated:* goals should be related to time scales.

In addition, goals should be agreed jointly by you and your subordinate. Generally employees are motivated to achieve goals when they have participated in setting them.

Most performance can be measured in terms of quantity, quality, time or cost. If, for some reason, the standards of performance cannot be expressed in measurable terms, such as a personal skill like communications, then you should spend time describing in detail the standard of performance required.

Examples of goals for the district sales manager are:

(a) Recruit four new sales staff before the end of March.
(b) Introduce product X to not less than 20 customers within four weeks of the product launch.
(c) Increase sales of product Y by 5% per quarter (in volume terms) over the coming year.

It is essential to have at least one goal stated for each key result area. Sometimes two or three goals are stated for each key result area.

Giving instructions

Instructions can be verbal or written. Verbal instructions have the great advantage that you can reinforce their importance through the vehicle of your non-verbal communication such as tone of voice, facial expression, gestures, etc. If you give a verbal instruction it might on occasions be helpful to follow it up in writing. Lengthy and complex instructions are always best expressed in writing. Bear the following in mind when giving instructions:

- What are your objectives in giving an instruction?
  What exact action do you want to initiate?

- Consider background factors such as:

  - the status/circumstances/motivation of the employee.

  - the present climate (hostile, friendly, stressful, etc.).

  - the complexity of the order.

- Decide the type of instruction:

  - Strong (direct instructions or commands, unilateral statements, non-negotiable instructions.)

  - Indirect (suggestions – the best orders are those that are constructed as if they were orders the receiver would have given himself or herself.)

  - Avoid weak instructions such as pleading.

- Give only necessary instructions and keep them brief, accurate and to the point (as the need arises and without delay). Too many can tend to confuse subordinates, while not enough can lead to a lack of direction from above.

- The content of your instruction will include WHO will do WHAT and WHEN with possibly WHERE, HOW, and WHY as appropriate.

- Know the consequences of NOT executing the order, and be ready to communicate this if necessary.

- Check that the instruction is understood – this is done best by asking the employee to say what he or she will do.

- Describe the outcomes and benefits of completing the task.

Improving employee performance

This model is an easy to follow guide to improving employee performance. It is based on the idea of catching the employee doing something right. For the employee it provides recognition and the satisfaction of knowing he or she is doing a good job.

- *Step 1* Give clear instructions
  Make sure that the instructions you give are clear and are understood by the employee. Agree the standard of performance which is required. Set goals.

- *Step 2* Monitor performance
  Depending on the job being done, devise some system for monitoring performance. There may be reports which allow you to measure performance against required standards or you may have to develop a measurement system.

- *Step 3* Recognize performance
  The most powerful recognition which you can give for employee performance is to stress your satisfaction verbally to the employee. There are many other ways in which you can reward performance. You should develop your own repertoire of rewards to reinforce performance.
  There are also ways in which you can recognize that the employee's performance has not been satisfactory. It is very important that when you are giving positive or negative feedback it occurs immediately after the performance, and the subordinate is fully aware of the reasons for it.

- *Step 4* Review
  The above three steps, particularly when repeated over time, have

the effect of improving employee performance since the goals can be raised as the employee's performance improves. You should keep an occasional check of performance to ensure that standards don't drop and bad habits don't creep in.

Delegating

All managers delegate tasks from time to time. You can only do so much yourself. The great advantage of delegation is that it releases time for you to move on to more important roles and tasks, such as planning and building up the department/business. In addition, delegation enriches the work of subordinates and prepares them for advancement.

- Analyse your current tasks to decide which ones can be delegated now or later on. Routine, programmed or fact finding tasks are the easiest to delegate. So are the detailed implementation of decisions already taken.

- A useful exercise is to analyse all paper work crossing your desk over a period and then ask yourself: can it be dealt with by someone else? One of the best ways is to arrange that paperwork reaches you partly or virtually completed.

- Delegate to subordinates who demonstrate potential for taking on more responsibility. Have they the right skills, confidence and motivation? You may need to prepare the person first with special coaching and counselling and if necessary, off-the-job training.

- Remember the principle: delegate to the lowest level possible, compatible with a reasonable chance of success.

- Weigh up the cost of delegating a task against the expected gains before you make the decision to delegate. Only delegate a vital task when you can be sure that it will be done on time and to the required standard. And when you delegate a task, keep in touch with the person regarding its progress.

- Sell the task and reassure the person that he or she can do it. If the increase in responsibility does not involve an increase in pay, you may need to show how it will prepare the person for future opportunities.

- Define the task (preferably in writing) and why it needs to be done. Discuss the deadline, the standard required, the resources available to carry it out (budget, staff, etc.). Discuss the authority the person has to make decisions, the problems that must be referrred back to you, the progress reports (if any) that should be produced and the precise form of the final report (recommendations) to be submitted. Ensure that there is sufficient time and resources for the person to have a reasonable chance of success.

- Don't delegate to the point where subordinates actually object or begin to fail to deliver successful results.

- Make it routine that subordinates give you regular feedback on how delegated matters are progressing. Allocate specific times when you can both go through the work together. Apart from this, leave them alone to get on with the job. Let them know your door is always open if they need your help at any time.

- Help subordinates to feel confident that you will back them as long as they have genuinely done their best.

- Reward success (verbal/written praise, financial rewards, comments in newsletters, public congratulations, symbolic gifts). But don't fail to criticize if necessary. Don't accept work which you know to be imperfect, to do so does not help the subordinate to grow.

- Finally achieve the correct balance between delegating too much work and not delegating enough.

Summary
- Pick one of your own tasks which is suitable for delegation.

- Select a subordinate.

- Coach/counsel them on the task.

- Agree success criteria.

- Monitor progress and support delegatee.

- Reward success/help failures.

- Pick another task.

Giving performance feedback

To improve employee performance it is essential to let employees know how you feel that are performing. This is performance feedback, one of the most powerful of all managerial skills.

Feedback is easier and more productive in situations of high mutual trust and confidence. Generally, it is easier to say 'I like what you are doing' than it is to say 'I do not like what you are doing'. You can overcome this difficulty through the development of mutual confidence, openness and trust between you and your subordinates. Managed in this way, feedback will help your staff to grow through helping them to see themselves as others see them.

- Positive feedback, catching people doing the right thing, is the most powerful form of feedback. Give far more positive feedback to your work group than negative feedback. Apart from the motivational effect, it also helps to build confidence and trust.

- Be alert to situations where an employee asks for feedback. It is easiest when the initiative comes from the other person.

- Give feedback at the earliest opportunity after the given behaviour.

- Give feedback in terms of the behaviour of the employee, not personality traits. Say, 'I am speaking to you because your report had five mistakes in it', not, 'You are careless when writing reports'. Don't say, 'You are a good worker', say 'Your output exceeded the required standard by 5 per cent, last week'.

- Don't give feedback which cannot be acted on – for example, a speech impediment, poor complexion, lack of intelligence or an innate aptitude.

- Check your feedback with the employee to ensure that it has been accurately and clearly understood. One way of doing this is to have the employee rephrase the feedback he or she has received to see if it corresponds with what you have in mind.

- Give the employee an opportunity to discuss how behaviour might be further improved.

- Phrase your feedback in non-threatening language so that the employee does not become defensive.

- When you are giving feedback to someone it helps the process if you demonstrate that you are open to feedback yourself.

- Sometimes it is better not to press for an immediate response to negative feedback. Give the employee a couple of days to consider what has been said.

- Normally you should set a follow-up date to review progress.

Recognizing progress

An employee who takes on additional work or new responsibilities benefits from encouragement. You should have regular, informal chats with the employee and recognize the progress which has been made.

- Tell the employee exactly what you wish to recognize.

- Let the employee know what progress has been made and how you expect it to continue in the future.

- Tell the employee how satisfied you are personally with the progress.

- Thank the employee for the effort which he or she is making to progress.

Recognizing above-average performance

Catching people doing the right thing is far more important than catching people doing the wrong thing. Always be on the lookout for opportunities to recognize above average performance. Use this guide when someone is making a real effort to correct a problem or where you feel above average performance needs to be recognized. Recognize immediately after the event. Don't save it up for a holiday.

- Tell the employee exactly what it is that you wish to recognize.

- Tell the employee the effects which this performance has on the work of your unit.

- Let the employee know how satisfied you feel about the performance. Let the employee know if other managers are aware of the above average performance. Explain how it reflects favourably on the employee.

- Do not allow the employee to use the opportunity to raise other issues, such as a salary increase, time off, etc. If a new topic is raised, set up a new meeting to discuss it.

Managing the poor performer

Before you talk to a subordinate about poor performance, the following questions are worth considering when planning your approach.

Consider the job
- Is the job too demanding/not demanding enough?

- Is the job badly designed.

- Does the employee have sufficient resources (money, time, staff) to do the job?

- How are others coping with similar jobs?

Consider the performance
- What is the standard of performance expected of the person? Is it realistic? Was the standard communicated to the person?

- Has the person the basic ability to do the job?

- Was the briefing/training adequate?

- Has feedback on performance already been given?

- Are there any other possible reasons for the poor performance (for example family, medical, peer group, etc.)?

- Is there documented proof of a performance discrepancy?

Decide on corrective action
- *Counsel.* Consider what counselling, coaching, training to give in order to reduce the performance discrepancy. Can the job be redesigned? How about relocation or job change?

- *Involve others*. Who else should be involved – other managers, the work group, personnel department, the union, etc?

- *Discipline*. Discipline for poor performance should be a last resort and must be in accordance with employment legislation. Relevant company procedures have to be checked with the personnel department.

Address the person
- Put the employee at ease.

- Look for agreement from the employee that there is a performance discrepancy and the extent of it, possibly by reference to historical data, written or unwritten norms, or by comparison with the peer group. Get agreement on responsibility for the discrepancy.

- Give the employee an opportunity to state his or her case and to suggest remedial action.

- Draw up an action plan together to reduce the discrepancy. This should include a time scale for action and a method of monitoring progress.

- Be firm but supportive throughout the interview.

- Always set a date for a follow-up meeting.

Performance appraisal

'How well am I doing?' Most employees want to know the answer to this fundamental question. An effective performance appraisal scheme, if it encourages a considerable sharing of views, will meet this need. Some schemes, however, are over-elaborate and have conflicting objectives. The best are simple and encourage an open dialogue between manager and employee. The discussion should reflect reviews throughout the year, and should contain no surprises for the employee.

- Prepare well before a meeting. Review the records of the last performance appraisal discussion. Review performance against goals previously agreed and ask the employee to prepare in the same way. Decide if there are any other issues you need to discuss. Decide on those issues you wish to emphasize.

- Set a mutually agreed date for the meeting. Describe the procedure to be followed. Arrange a location where you will not be interrupted. Make sure you both have enough time.

- Put the employee at ease.

- Give the employee an opportunity to describe how he or she feels the job is progressing.

- Examine together how well previously set goals in key result areas of the job were achieved. Were the standards met and were they achieved on time? What improvement is needed?

- Give recognition for fully satisfactory performance and emphasize above average performance.

- Discuss not more than two areas where performance needs to be improved. Explain why improvement is necessary and set a follow-up date.

- Agree new goals/standards of performance and an action plan to achieve them.

- Discuss training needs. What help does the subordinate need to achieve the new performance standards: help from you; from others, from courses?

- Update the job description if necessary.

- Document the outcome and put it on the employee's file.

- Do not discuss salary reviews at this meeting.

- Conclude by summarizing what you think the interview has achieved. Try to end on a positive note, the appraisee feeling up rather than down.

- Fix the date for a follow-up meeting.

Rewarding performance

The best way to ensure that an employee continues to perform well is to recognize good performance in some way. The most powerful way is for you to recognize performance verbally soon after the event. Sometimes, something more tangible is necessary. Unfortunately, many of the formal organizational rewards, such as promotion or salary increase, may not be available or appropriate. You can develop your own lists of ways to reward performance. Some suggestions are set down below:

- *Tokens of appreciation*
    - Buy a cup of coffee.
    - Pay for lunch.
    - Give tickets for theatre.
    - Improve office facilities.
    - Help with some project.
    - Pay for overtime.
    - Recommend for special award.

- *Personal safeguards*
    - Provide some additional guarantees to the employee regarding employment, etc.
    - Find out from the employee if he or she feels vulnerable in any way (for example, lack of specialist training), and take appropriate action.

- *Social recognition*
    - Spend more time with the employee.
    - Involve the employee in your work.
    - Encourage the employee to participate more in the organization.
    - Reduce any anti-social effect of the employee's work (such as working weekends).

- Introduce the employee to visitors to your work unit.
- Socialize with the employee.
- Provide support/assistance to the employee.

- *Public recognition*
  - Praise the employee.
  - Praise the employee in front of others.
  - Get your manager to praise the employee.
  - Write to the employee (copy on file).
  - Write to the employee at home.
  - Recognize the employee's contribution in your house magazine.

- *Opportunities for personal development*
  - Give the employee greater opportunities to define his or her own job.
  - Give the employee additional time or resources to complete a pet project.
  - Allow an employee time off to take a course of study.

Discussing a salary change

Salary is the most important part of an employee's remuneration. Accordingly, employees place a big emphasis on changes to their salaries. Every time a change occurs, such as an annual review, an upgrading or a promotion, you should sit down with the employee and discuss the basis for the change. This approach is particularly true for increases based on an employee's performance. An employee should see the relationship between the salary change and his or her performance. The employee is not only more likely to perform better but will also have more job satisfaction knowing that his or her performance has been recognized. Weaker performers are also more likely to respond to the pay for performance system. An additional advantage of a good discussion is that it reduces the impact of the rumour mill with regard to salary changes.

- Explain to the employee the purpose of the discussion.

- Tell the employee the amount of the increase (actual and %) and the date on which it takes effect.

- Explain the basis of the calculation of the increase.

- Listen carefully to the employee's reaction.

- If appropriate, explain again the basis of the calculation. Focus on the employee's ability to influence increases through performance.

- End the discussion by thanking the employee for his or her efforts and express your confidence with regard to future performance.

Coaching

Coaching is a highly practical form of on-the-job training. It is the personal help or guided experience a manager gives subordinates. Ideally it should be a continuous process. It may also, however, be incorporated into both counselling and appraisal sessions. The main thrust of coaching is to help your subordinates improve their performance, or deal with problems, by goal-setting and feedback.

Here are some broad guidelines for the coach:

- Adjust coaching to the individual needs of each subordinate. No two people are alike, so have a plan for each subordinate's development. Give them progressively more difficult and challenging assignments/specific projects. They might however, need some specific training course beforehand to carry out these tasks.

- Ask yourself:
  - Does their job and the way it is being done place real demands on them?
  - How will I make the job more challenging for them?
  - Are there areas of my job I can delegate to them?

- Ask them questions about their work progress.
  - Have you any idea how you might have handled the assignment differently?
  - What problems did you face?
  - How could I have helped you more?
  - Do you think there might be another way of looking at the problem?

- Encourage them to seek out information, to come up with their own solutions and to propose action. As far as possible, give them the authority to make the final decision and to implement any action.

- Agree and summarize future action. Do they fully understand what has been discussed, and can they explain to you what action they will take?

- Monitor performance and give regular feedback. Finally, encourage your subordinates to find time to reflect on their work as a learning experience. Let them know that you are willing to help.

- If appropriate, set a review date.

Career counselling

Career counselling takes place between a subordinate and his or her boss or with a careers/personnel specialist. Some subordinates need counselling more than others (for example, 'fast track' employees). As well as assisting the employee, it is a very useful part of company manpower planning. Employees may have skills and interests which are currently under utilized. Here are some steps in the career counselling process:

- Start with the reality of where the person is now. Make sure you are fully conversant with the employee's background and track record.

- Encourage the employee to talk freely about what he or she wants to do with his or her career and why. How does he or she see the future?

- What alternative career paths are there? Encourage the employee to 'freewheel' ideas, to keep options open.

- Ask the employee to identify strengths and weaknesses, and ask what action the employee intends to take which would equip him or her for the future. What commitment is he or she prepared to make?

- Let the person know that career counselling does not assume that a new job role will definitely be provided, nor does it guarantee a career path or promotion. Be open, honest and sympathetic, but do not build false hopes.

- Draw up a development plan together for the coming year, and get commitment to it. It is essential that the subordinate does not have unrealistic expectations regarding his or her career.

- Remember that career counselling can help the employee, but the employee has the ultimate responsibility for his or her own development and growth.

6 Employee Relations

There is always a potential conflict between organizational goals and the personal goals and expectations of individual members of your work group. If this is not resolved, employee relations difficulties arise. Such difficulties may result in poor performance, in increases in absenteeism and employee turnover, and also in dysfunctional behaviour by some members of the work group. The management of employee relations is therefore part of the manager's job.

It is better to take a proactive approach than to wait until a problem arises. Such an approach addresses three issues: employee involvement; job design; and employee concerns. It enables you to align, as far as practicable, organizational goals with the personal goals of employees. It also helps you to manage expectations, so that employees find out which are unrealistic for members of your work group.

Of course, problems do arise from time to time. There are two types of employee relations problems: the problem employee and the employee problem. In the former case, the objective is to put the employee back on course with the minimum of difficulty to either the employee or the work group. Very often a breach of some work rule is involved and disciplinary action is required. An important principle comes into play. It is that the purpose of disciplinary action is to correct behaviour through discipline rather than to punish for wrongdoing. It is important that in your actions you comply with legislative requirements and are perceived by other members of the work group as acting fairly.

Grievances arise when an employee's expectations have not been met. They should be seen as an opportunity for you to show the same concern for people's expectations as you would hope them to show for the achievement of work goals. You show that concern in two ways. Firstly, you follow a procedure which gives the employee a fair chance to make his or her case before an appropriate person. Secondly, the problem is dealt with in a win–win way, so that every effort is made to resolve the employee's problem without jeopardizing the goals of the work group.

Do not wait for a problem to arise before addressing employee relations issues. Practices such as counselling and management by walking about enable you to be proactive. This approach is explained in the final guide in this section.

Managing employee relations

Some managers see the responsibility for employee relations resting elsewhere in the organization, such as with the personnel staff. What successful managers know is that, within their own work unit, they have responsibility for and benefit from managing employee relations. By being proactive in this area, they improve employee productivity and job satisfaction.

The reason that employee relations issues arise is that there is a potential conflict between the goals of the organization (for example profit, cost control, flexibility) and the goals of its employees (for example increased earnings, job satisfaction and personal growth). A positive approach to employee relations reconciles company goals and employee goals. It addresses three areas: employee involvement, job design, and a concern for employees. Review your management of these areas to improve employee relations in your work unit.

Involvement
The purpose of involvement is to create a sense of oneness between company goals and employee goals. It requires a considerable commitment on the part of the manager. It eliminates the Them and Us syndrome, and makes employees more flexible and amenable to change.

- Keep employees informed of developments within the organization. Get rid of the Need to Know rule and communicate as much as possible.

- Pass on all information that you receive which is not strictly confidential.

- Carry out debriefings after any important meetings you attend.

- Conduct regular (weekly/fortnightly/monthly) two-way communication sessions with all your staff.

- Inform all staff of important decisions which you are taking in your work area.

- Involve all staff in the problem solving processes (problem identification, solution generation) in matters which affect them or their work areas.

- Involve employees in decision making processes where the acceptability of the decision is as important as the quality of the decision.

- Ensure that employees share in the success of your work unit. Give credit where it is due. Celebrate successes. Make sure everyone knows what has been achieved and who has achieved it.

Job design
- Ensure that jobs are challenging and interesting (so far as practical) for the employee. Develop a work environment where people can feel proud about the work they do, the area in which they work (cleanliness and decoration are important), and the respect which is shown to employees and other people with whom they come in contact.

- Establish a clear sense of direction for your work group. Have clear goals and standards of performance for the total work group and for each employee in it.

- Develop measures of accountability so that every employee knows how he or she is doing against required goals.

Concern for employees
- Show scrupulous integrity and consistency in your dealings with employees.

- Be proactive in addressing employee concerns before they give rise to conflict. Be visible and accessible: 'management by walking about'.

- Be fair in dealings with all employees – for example, not showing favouritism.

- Establish standards of behaviour which are a source of pride to employees.

- Enforce rules firmly, consistently and impersonally.

- Keep rules to a minimum.

- Have effective formal and informal employee problem solving (grievance) procedures.

- Use your skills as a manager to encourage conformity to rules rather than by using discipline.

- However, be prepared to use an acceptable disciplinary procedure to deal with employees who will not conform to work rules.

Rules about rules

Rules set out the minimum standards of performance or behaviour which an organization or a manager will accept. For example, most factories require employees to operate in a safe manner. However, the safety rules, the minimum standard of performance, in one factory may differ from those in another. It is not sufficient to lay down a rule, you must enforce it. A rule which is not enforced will lapse, however clearly it is written down. Here are some rules about rules:

- Rules should be as few in number as possible, otherwise you will spend your time enforcing rules and employees will feel that they are unduly restricted.

- They should be reasonable in content.

- They should be known and understood. The legal dictum 'ignorance of the law is no defence' does not apply in the workplace.

- Rules should be acceptable. If you have too many rules that are unacceptable, you will not be able to enforce them all and they will lapse.

- Rules should be fairly and consistently applied to all employees, at all levels in the organization.

The disciplinary meeting

A disciplinary meeting is one of the most difficult meetings a manager has to face. It often takes place in an emotionally charged atmosphere with bad feelings on the part of the employee. In this environment the manager has quite an amount to achieve.

Results required
- The offence must be established.

- The correct discipline must be administered.

- The consequences of failure to improve by the employee must be made clear.

- The employee should make a commitment to improve/not to repeat the offence.

- The disciplinary procedure must be followed and accurate records maintained.

Be fair
You want to be considered a fair manager and employees expect no less of you. Should your disciplinary action ever be reviewed by a tribunal it will not only look at the conduct of the employee, it will investigate whether the action you took was fair. You must ensure that you handle disciplinary cases fairly.

- Fully investigate the offence, the greater the offence the greater the investigation required.

- Follow closely the disciplinary procedure.

- Make a clear statement of the offence.

- Give the employee an opportunity to state his or her case.

- If provided for in the procedure or in cases of serious disciplinary action, offer the employee the right to representation.

- Make sure that the rules were known and had been consistently enforced previously.

- Give due consideration to the employee's side of the case.

- Make sure the punishment fits the crime.

- Give the employee a right to appeal, and explain the procedure to be followed.

The right procedure

Follow this procedure for a disciplinary meeting and you will go a long way to ensuring that any disciplinary action you take will be fair and be seen to be fair. Before the meeting check the facts and the company rules. For serious matters consult with colleagues concerning procedure and precedent.

- Put the employee at ease.

- State the reason for the meeting.

- If appropriate, state the right to representation, for instance by a union or a colleague.

- Outline the offence.

- Ask for explanation/the employee's case.

- Reply to the employee's case.

- Give the reason for disciplinary action.

- Define the action.

- Seek commitment to improvement/outline consequence of failure to improve.

- Explain the appeals procedure.

Disciplinary penalties

The appropriate disciplinary penalty will differ from organization to organization. The penalties you administer must be appropriate, follow procedure, and be accepted as legitimate in your organization. For example, some organizations provide for the withholding of privileges under their disciplinary procedure. If this is not acceptable in your organization, it is wrong for you to do so.

The verbal abuse of an employee, like putting him or her down, should not be employed. Finally, make sure that when you administer a penalty you link it very clearly to the offence otherwise the employee may feel victimized.

For minor offences it is usual for the manager to have an informal chat 'off the record' with the employee. For serious offences the manager will usually move directly to action such as a final warning or suspension. The usual progression of penalties is as follows:

- Caution.

- Written warning.

- Withdrawal of privileges, such as a salary increment.

- Final warning.

- Suspension with pay (used during investigations).

- Suspension without pay.

- Disciplinary transfer.

- Dismissal.

Grievance procedure

The grievance procedure serves a number of purposes. It assists in the resolution of employee problems. It balances manager-subordinate relations making it legitimate for the subordinate to sit down with the manager to discuss issues. It allows the subordinate to go above his or her manager to have a problem resolved.

An effective grievance procedure also prevents the build up of issues and conflicts, and is a source of job satisfaction to employees. For this reason many organizations provide a number of different procedures, such as an open-door procedure, a peer grievance procedure, etc. A grievance procedure also functions as an appeal against disciplinary action.

A grievance procedure has three main stages, although each stage may have a number of steps.

- *Stage 1* Preliminary review
  Most procedures require that employees raise issues with their immediate superiors and, only when a proper discussion has taken place, can the issue go for a formal hearing.

- *Stage 2* A formal hearing
  The employee records the issue in writing as a grievance and discusses it with his or her manager.

- *Stage 3* Appeal
  If an employee fails to obtain satisfaction at the formal hearing he or she is entitled to appeal the manager's decision to a higher manager. For serious matters, it is usual to allow a number of appeals; for example, in the case of dismissal an appeal to the chief executive is usually provided for.

Grievance meetings

Whether you are the manager involved at the preliminary review, the formal hearing or an appeal, the following procedure is of value in conducting the meeting:

- Put the employee at ease.

- Ask the employee for details of the grievance.

- Listen carefully and probe to get the full facts of the case.

- Ask for suggestions with regard to how the grievance can be resolved.

- Review the grievance and ways of resolving it. If necessary, check with a colleague regarding precedents and procedures.

- Agree an action plan or further appeal. The action plan may involve you discussing the resolution of the grievance with other managerial staff.

- Get a follow-up date either for the appeal or to review whether the action plan has resolved the grievance.

Counselling

From time to time managers have to take on the role of counsellor. This helps the manager build a strong relationship with subordinates, and improves employee performance at the same time. Here are some guidelines:

- Have the meeting private and free from interruptions.

- Avoid awkward barriers (desk/space). Put the employee at ease and reassure him or her that the discussion is confidential.

- Encourage the employee to describe the facts of the situation. Use open and probing questions to get the full story.

- Be a good listener and don't make any assumptions. As you listen, don't convey any indications of impatience, such as looking at your watch.

- Be calm and don't show any dismay at what the employee reveals.

- When the facts have been set out, try to get the employee to say how he or she feels about them.

- Assist the employee to analyse the situation.

- Don't offer any criticism or make decisions for the employee. Instead, help the employee to see the decision for himself or herself through questioning, focusing, and through generating alternative lines of action for consideration.

- Assess when the employee needs specialist help and, if so, encourage him or her to visit an appropriate advisor or agency.

Management by walking about

One of the most interesting and powerful, yet simple, employee relations techniques is managing by walking about. It is designed as an antidote to the sense of remoteness and alienation sometimes felt by employees in large organizations. It brings the manager into regular contact with his or her staff and the work they do. Properly conducted, it benefits both manager and staff.

Managers need to know what is happening in their areas, not just at their immediate level, but also at the levels below that. They must know what their subordinates are doing, what they feel about their performance, training, working conditions, etc. Staff benefit from the opportunity to discuss these matters, and to learn at first hand about the running of the operation. Your visits should be thought out. Merely wandering around will not work, and may create the wrong impression.

- Make regular visits to all parts of your operation.

- Don't wait for a crisis before meeting the workforce.

- Explain to your line managers the reason for your visits, and assure them that you will not undermine their authority.

- Meet and talk to as many people as possible.

- Encourage openness by being open and supportive in your own comments.

- Be aware and informed of significant issues.

- Look for opportunities to encourage good behaviour.

- Tackle areas of concern, either employee problems or problems with employees, through the line.

- Follow up action items promptly.

7 Problem Solving and Decision Making

One of the main characteristics looked for in a manager is a good problem solving and decision making ability. These terms are often used as though they were interchangeable, yet it is helpful to think of them as distinct activities. Decision making is required when the problem solving process suggests a number of possible courses of action.

It is frequently assumed that problem solving and decision making ability is innate, or that it develops with experience. Some managers do seem to have more natural ability in this regard. However, the tendency nowadays is to encourage the use of a variety of very good techniques.

The effect of using these techniques is not only superior problem solving and decision making, but also the involvement of staff at all levels in the organization. Very often, the involvement of staff results in superior problem solving.

A problem is a deviation or gap between desired and actual performance, for instance in quality, customer service, outputs, absenteeism. There is an important distinction to be made between two different types of problem. One type is the routine, repetitive sort that managers are called to deal with on a day-to-day basis, for which there are usually corporate procedures, guidelines or precedents. Non-programmed problems require a creative problem solving mechanism, and they tend to be one-off problems. They include problems which are being tackled for the first time; problems which no longer respond to the old remedies; or, more obviously, problems in inventing some product or service.

Different types of problem require different approaches. There are a number of techniques which are helpful in dealing with problems. Two of these, the cause-and-effect diagram and the Pareto methods, are described in this section. For non-programmed problems, special techniques which overcome barriers to creativity are required. Again, two techniques are described: brainstorming and the nominal group techniques.

The last group of guides in this section are aids to decision making. They include guides to overcoming procrastination and to help you be decisive. The last guide will help your decision making when there are decisions which must be taken in sequence. The decision tree technique enables you to see the full sequence of choices simultaneously. In certain cases, we can ascribe a numeric value to alternative courses of action.

Problem solving

Most managers use the terms 'problem solving' and 'decision making' interchangeably. Yet it is helpful to think of decision making as a distinct activity. The manager makes a decision whenever he or she makes a choice from a number of alternatives. Problem solving involves a seven-stage process to determine the nature and cause of some deviation or gap between desired and actual performance. It can be seen as a seven-step process:

- *Problem identification:* does a problem exist? What is the nature of the problem? How important is it? Can it be stated in another way?

- *Gaining information:* what information is needed to solve the problem? What data is available? What additional information is required? Ask questions relating to who, what, where, when and why.

- *Generating solutions:* what kind of problem is this? Is this solution provided for in company procedures or is creative problem solving required?

- *Evaluating solutions:* generate criteria (for example, financial, time, precedent for determining which solution will be adopted). Evaluate possible solutions against the criteria.

- *Selection:* choose the most suitable solution and, if appropriate, communicate it.

- *Implementation:* plan and implement the selected action.

- *Follow up:* monitor the implementation of the solution and take appropriate action to ensure that the problem does not recur.

Types of problem

The manager must differentiate between two main types of problems requiring very different forms of problem solving.

Programmed problems
These are the routine problems which managers face in their daily work. Although they may be complex, the solutions can be found by following precedent, procedures, systems or company practice. Examples include machine breakdown, a salary decision, developing a budget, or meeting a tight deadline.

Management science contains many techniques – like linear programming, queueing theory and decision tree techniques – for assisting managers in dealing with programmed problems. Computers also help managers in dealing with quite complex numerical problems. In general, programmed problems are routine, can be laid out in advance and have a single correct solution.

Non-programmed problems
From time to time managers will be faced with problems for which there is no system or procedure for determining the right course of action. A creative solution must be found. Examples of non-programmed problems include inventing a new product, developing a marketing campaign, or managing a crisis. The most commonly used method of creative problem solving is brainstorming. Other methods are suggested below.

Cause-and-effect diagrams

Just as it is important to distinguish between the symptoms and the disease before commencing medical treatment, so a manager must be careful to distinguish between the causes of a problem and their effect. The effect is the manifestation of a problem, such as a 10% increase in rejects during May. An effective analysis will identify the root cause(s) of the problem so that appropriate action can be taken. A cause-and-effect diagram, also known as a fishbone diagram, will help you understand the relationship between the different factors which may have contributed to the problem.

Label the problem
The first step is to label the problem correctly. You label a problem by expressing the effect it has, in sufficient detail, so that other people can identify it. Ideally, labels should answer questions such as who, what, how, how many, when (for example, during July absenteeism increased by 3% among night shift personnel)?

Identify the factors
What are the main stages or factors involved in the process? For many problems you will consider people, systems, materials and equipment. Refer to flow diagrams or work processes.

Draw the diagram
Prepare a fishbone diagram (see Figure 7.1). Write the label in the box. Identify the factors which contribute to the effect. Link the factors to the centre line with 'bones'. Along those bones identify the possible causes of the problem. If appropriate, use the brainstorming techniques later in this section to identify possible causes.

Identify the root causes
• Identify the most probable root causes.

150

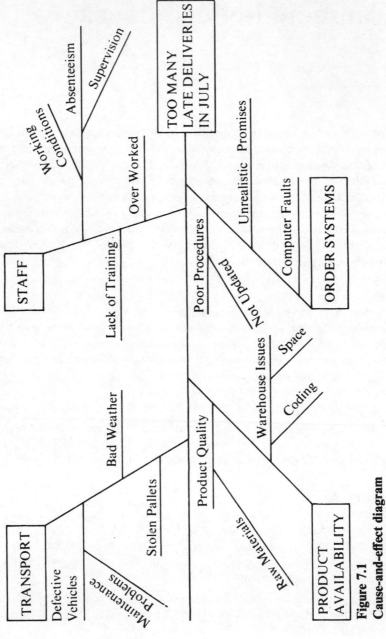

Figure 7.1
Cause-and-effect diagram

- Collect data on the most likely causes.

- Test the most likely causes.

- If appropriate, use the Pareto method to identify the most significant causes.

Pareto analysis

Very often a recurring problem comprises several different problems, or results from a variety of causes. In such cases a Pareto analysis can be helpful in organizing data to show the most significant factors affecting the situation. It is based on the 80–20 principle – for example, 80% of problems result from 20% of causes. If you want to make an impact in tackling a problem, concentrate on the 20% of factors causing 80% of the problems.

The Pareto principle has many applications in business. You may want to investigate a problem under a variety of headings

What:	what are the different causes of the problem?
When:	during which periods are problems most likely to arise?
Where:	where do the problems most frequently occur?
Who:	who are the people or groups who experience the most problems?
How:	how does the problem happen?
How much:	which problems cost the most?

A Pareto diagram is a bar chart in which the bars are arranged in descending order from the left (see Figure 7.2). There are eight steps involved in setting up the diagram:

(1) Correct as much data as you can indicating the nature and frequency of the occurrence.
(2) Determine the categories under which you will analyse the data.
(3) Allocate the frequency of the occurrence to the different categories.
(4) Calculate the frequency in percentages.
(5) Prepare a bar chart with the left axis for data and the right axis for the percentage of the total.

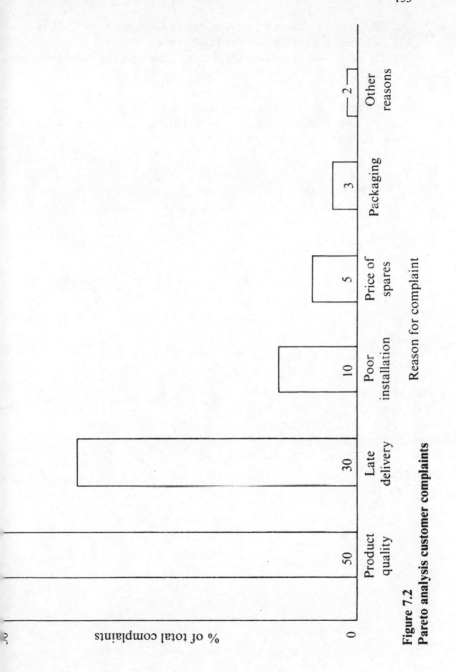

Figure 7.2
Pareto analysis customer complaints

(6) Prepare the chart with bars in decreasing order from the left.
(7) Check the bar chart for the Pareto effect.
(8) If the Pareto effect is evident, take action on the most prevalent factors.

If the Pareto effect is not evident (the chart is too flat), repeat the analysis under different categories so that significant causes are eventually identified and can be acted upon.

Creative problem solving

Most organizations require their employees to act in a predictable way. They have procedures, rules, precedents and norms to be followed. As a consequence, individual employees tend to curb their creative side. Managers wish to appear rational, logical and analytical. Thus, individually and organizationally, there are barriers to creativity. Most times this is good, but there are occasions on which the manager must use creative problem solving processes to get a creative response from his or her work group.

Creative problem solving
These are four stages in the creative process:

- *Preparation:* clarify the problem. State it and restate it in as many different ways as possible – for instance, the shop has no customers, customers don't like shopping here, customers prefer to shop elsewhere. Collect available information and data. Select and brief a problem solving group.

- *Reflection:* if time permits, allow for a period of reflection. Take a coffee break, or better still sleep on the problem overnight. It is surprising how often a solution 'presents' itself during reflection.

- *Generating solutions:* sometimes a single solution will stand out as the way forward. This occurs when the group gains an insight into the problem. It is frequently accompanied by the 'Aha' feeling experienced by a group which realizes intuitively that it has solved the problem. More frequently, many solutions must be generated before one is adjudged to be the most appropriate.

- *Verification:* during this stage the whole group uses its experience and judgement to evaluate proposed solutions against criteria such as legality, cost and practicality.

Generating solutions

Of their nature, creative solutions do not follow conventional wisdom or logic. They will not be discovered unless organizational and individual barriers to creativity are overcome. The fundamental rule is to separate idea generation from evaluation. Whatever technique is chosen, you must ensure that people feel free to propose solutions without fear of criticism. There are four guidelines to be followed:

- *Go for quantity:* generate as many feasible solutions as possible. Sometimes a problem is solved by combining a number of solutions.

- *Suspend judgement:* don't allow any criticism or evaluation of ideas until as many solutions as possible have been generated.

- *Freewheel:* encourage all sorts of ideas. Allow the group to dream and fantasize. Encourage wild and silly ideas.

- *Cross fertilize:* depending on the process being followed, encourage participants to build on each other's ideas.

Become familiar with the many different creative problem solving techniques. Guidelines for using the brainstorming and nominal group techniques are included in this book.

Group problem solving

Research indicates that problem solving in groups tends to be better than problem solving by individuals. This not too surprising result comes from the pooled information which a group generates, and from the interaction of group members in effective groups. However, managers often prefer to make decisions themselves to save time, to save expense and to ensure that their own preferred decisions are taken.

There are other reasons why managers sometimes prefer to make their own decisions. Not all groups have the ability or capability to solve problems. In general, managers should consider five factors when deciding whether to involve their work groups in decision making:

- *Quality of the decision:* how important is it that optimum decision is made or are there a number of decisions which can resolve the problem?

- *Acceptability of the decision:* to what extent is it important that the work group agree with and accept a decision?

- *Information:* do members of the work group have the information required to solve the problem?

- *Work group:* to what extent is the work group trained, experienced and motivated to make the best decision?

- *Speed and expense:* is it important that a decision be made quickly, and does the nature of the problem warrant the expense of group problem solving?

Brainstorming

Brainstorming is the most widely used creative problem solving technique. It is very effective in generating a large number of ideas. It is not unusual to generate more than a hundred ideas in 20 minutes. Unfortunately, the technique is frequently abused by session leaders not following the correct procedure; by allowing criticism during the brainstorming stage, for example.

- *Stating the problem:* the leader of the brainstorming session states the problem and explains the brainstorming process to participants. A brief general discussion ensures common understanding of the problem.

- *Restating the problem:* participants propose possible restatements of the problem following a 'In how many ways . . .?' format. 'In how many ways can customers be made to feel welcome?' This format encourages contributions from the group at the next stage. Depending on the nature of the problem, between five and ten restatements should be proposed, and one or two of them adopted for brainstorming.

- *Brainstorming:* the purpose of this stage is to generate as many ideas as possible. Quantity not quality is required. Participants should be reminded not to evaluate ideas and the session leader should ensure that evaluation doesn't occur. Ideas are recorded on flipcharts which are kept in view throughout the whole session to encourage participants to build on each other's ideas. The leader energizes the group by setting goals (only 15 more to reach 200) and by encouraging wild and offbeat ideas.

    When ideas begin to dry up, a coffee break may provide a suitable reflection period after which new ideas will be forthcoming. Suggesting ideas, encouraging quiet participants and asking the participants to build on previously stated ideas are all ways to maintain the free flow of ideas.

- *Evaluation:* if possible, allow a time gap between the generation of ideas and the evaluation process. Use this time to group ideas into manageable categories (20–40 items each), and to agree criteria (practicality, time, cost, etc.) for evaluating each category. Aim to select the three or four best ideas in each category for detailed evaluation. Eliminate unworkable ideas and record the remainder for future consideration.

Nominal group technique

This process is an important modification of the brainstorming technique. In it, group members suggest ideas independently. It is most appropriate when some participants might not respond well to the focal interaction involved in the brainstorming process. Strong personalities cannot dominate the nominal group technique.

- A group of not more than eight members is selected.

- The session leader defines the problem using a 'In how many ways...?' format. For example, 'In how many ways can this department reduce costs?'

- Participants silently record their ideas for resolving the problem.

- On a round-robin basis, participants state their ideas one at a time. Each idea is recorded on a flipchart in a few words. The round-robin process continues until all ideas are recorded.

- Ideas are discussed for clarification and evaluation.

- Decision making is by secret independent voting. The result is determined by the rank order of votes.

Groupthink

Effective problem solving in groups is often affected by a phenomenon known as groupthink. It occurs when group members are unduly influenced to achieve a consensus, or to be seen to abide by established beliefs and values that they do not give due consideration to alternative courses of action. It is found in highly cohesive groups, and results in overemphasis on conformity at the expense of realistic appraisal.

Symptoms of groupthink
A fundamental characteristic of groupthink is lack of objectivity and the suppression of independent ideas. There are other symptoms:

- Over optimism that the group knows all the right answers.

- The rejection of ideas and negative feedback from outside the group.

- A strong sense of the inherent morality of the group's position.

- Negative stereotyping of anyone who opposes the group's viewpoint.

- Group members keeping their views to themselves.

- A core of group members who shield the group from adverse information.

- Exclusion of independent expert advice.

Prevention of groupthink
Groups can avoid groupthink by encouraging the expression of minority and unpopular viewpoints, and by ensuring the thorough examination of the advantages and disadvantages of different courses of action.

- Encourage all group members to state their views and raise objections.

- Invite outside experts to participate at critical meetings.

- Appoint a 'devil's advocate' to identify problems and to suggest alternatives.

- Use sub-groups to examine alternative actions.

- Encourage dominant personalities to maintain an impartial stance during initial discussions.

Avoiding procrastination

Procrastinating managers delay making minor decisions. As a manager you are paid to make and be seen to make decisions. Remember that you will never have 100% certainty about most situations facing you. Decision making requires you to be courageous. It requires an act of faith in your own ability.

- Determine the criteria on which you will make your decision.

- Avoid being unduly influenced by others. Ask yourself what your gut feeling tells you about this decision.

- Don't spend time and energy agonizing over minor decisions when there is not much difference between the alternatives.

- Avoid getting bogged down in details. Keep your eyes on the basics.

- Get started on the 'doable' parts of a task, even when it is not possible to do the total task. This is the Swiss Cheese technique – it puts big holes in your work.

- Stick by your decision, unless some new facts come to light.

- Be prepared to defend your decision.

- Remember that procrastination in minor decisions will tire you, frustrate others and sap your energy.

- It is often better to make the wrong minor decision quickly than to wait for the right answer to come along.

Being decisive

In his autobiography, Lee Iacocca, the CEO of Chrysler says: 'If I had to sum up in one word the qualities that make a good manager, I'd say it all comes down to decisiveness. You can use the fanciest computers in the world and you can gather all the charts and numbers, but in the end you have to bring all your information together, set up a timetable, and act.' Follow this procedure to become a more decisive manager:

- Analyse major decisions into 'pros' and 'cons'. Write down two lists facing each other on a single sheet of paper and see where the decision lies.

- Ask yourself what is the worst that can happen if anything goes wrong? It will rarely prove to be quite as disastrous as you fear.

- Establish life and work guidelines for yourself and judge decisions against these criteria.

- What would (name some authority) do in these circumstances? Perhaps search for the solution in reference books, trade magazines, etc., or ask someone for help.

- Delay the decision for a short period (4–24 hours) to allow time for insight from your subconscious mind.

- Jot down the problem on a postcard in the form of a question demanding an answer and carry it with you in your pocket. Look at it several times during the day expecting the answer to come. Believe that it will.

- Finally, once you have made your decision, banish it from your mind and don't keep going back over it unless new information comes to light.

- Try hard to make the decision work.

Decision tree technique

A decision tree is a means of identifying a range of courses of action and displaying them to aid decision making. It is particularly appropriate when a number of decisions must be made in sequence. For example, if your computer system is inadequate, you might have to decide whether to upgrade your existing system or to purchase a new one. That decision would be followed by other decisions regarding hardware, software, choice of suppliers, etc. (see Figure 7.3).

A further advantage of the decision tree method is that once the alternative courses of action have been identified, it is possible in some cases to calculate a value for each alternative. To do this you need to know the cost of each alternative, an estimate of the probability of its success and the value of a success for each alternative. Sophisticated, yet simple to operate, computer programs are available to help in calculating these values. An example of an investment decision is set out in Figure 7.4.

Setting up the decision tree
The decision tree is set up in the following way. A square indicates that a decision must be made. A circle indicates a chance event. The probability of the event occurring is bracketed.

- Enter the first decision.

- Mark the end of each decision option by either a circle or a square.

- Continue the process with either events or decisions until you reach a final position.

- Enter available information onto the chart so that all the information required for a decision appears.

■ indicates a decision.

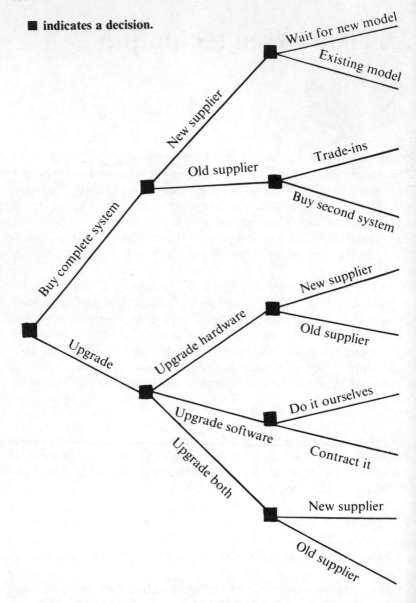

Figure 7.3
Decision tree analysis – computer system renewal.

167

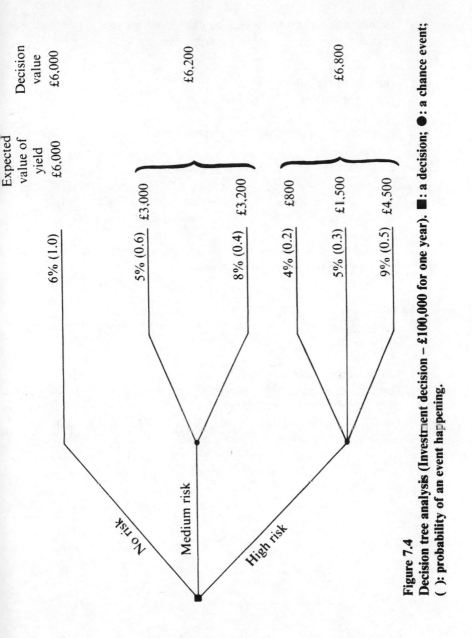

Figure 7.4
Decision tree analysis (Investment decision – £100,000 for one year). ■ : a decision; ● : a chance event; ( ): probability of an event happening.

- If the decision sequence can be calculated numerically, enter the appropriate values onto the decision tree.

Calculation of the value

- Enter the cost of each decision option.

- Estimate the probability of each possible outcome from a decision.

- Estimate the value of each decision outcome.

- Calculate the expected value for each outcome by multiplying the benefit of the outcome by the probability of its occurrence.

- Decisions can be compared by adding the expected values related to the possible outcomes for each decision.

Example

You have £100,000 to invest for one year, and you have the choice of three funds any of which seems suitable:

Fund A gives a fixed yield of 6%.
Fund B has two possible outcomes: a probability $P = 0.6$ of a 5% yield, and $P = 0.4$ of an 8% yield.
Fund C has three possible outcomes: $P = 0.2$ of a 4% yield, $P = 0.3$ of a 5% yield and $P = 0.5$ of a 9% yield.

The expected values of the funds are shown in Table 7.5.

Table 7.5
Example showing expected yields of three suitable funds

	Yield	Probability	Expected value	Decision value
Fund A	6%	1.0	£6,000	£6,000
Fund B	5%	0.6	£3,000	
	8%	0.4	£3,200	£6,200
Fund C	4%	0.2	£800	
	5%	0.3	£1,500	
	9%	0.5	£4,500	£6,800

The right decision is to invest in Fund C so long as you can tolerate some risk of a yield of 4%. Your expected yield is the highest of the three funds.

8 Meetings

Many managers complain about the number of meetings they must attend. Some days seem to consist of little more than a series of meetings. You often hear people remark that they did no work because of the meetings they had to attend. Usually, what they are complaining about is not their attendance at meetings but the unproductive nature of many of them. As a manager you should know how to manage meetings so that people attending them feel that they are productive and worthwhile. You also need to know how to identify what is going wrong during unsatisfactory meetings.

The key to a successful meeting lies in achieving the right combination of content and process. You must consider not only what is being discussed, but how it is being discussed. The guides in this section take you through the various process issues so that content can be dealt with effectively to the satisfaction of everyone attending meetings.

The final guide in this section is an aid to anyone involved in managing a complex organizational meeting such as a conference. Because of the high profile of such large meetings and their irregular occurrence, it is important that not only are the content and process issues tackled, but that the administrative arrangements are professionally carried out.

Taking the chair

Meetings are necessary in order to bring together everyone who needs to be informed or who has the required expertise to get things done. The test of a meeting is how efficiently the participants work together to complete its task. Your role as chairperson is to manage the meeting. You use procedures to guide this process. Here are some guidelines:

Before the meeting
- Draw up the agenda. Decide on the number of items feasible in the time available.

- Give adequate notice of the meeting and its objectives. Check the availability of participants. Circulate the agenda in good time before the meeting.

- Check the facilities (lighting, heating, ventilation, flip charts, projectors, etc.).

- Have copies of documents available for committee members, if required.

Start the meeting
- Check whether a quorum is present (if the rules require a quorum).

- Welcome the participants and express appreciation for attendance. Introduce new participants. Ask if apologies have been received. Arrange for someone to take minutes.

- Read minutes of last meeting.

- State the objectives of the meeting. Set a time limit, if appropriate.

- Clarify the roles of people present, if necessary.

- Clarify items on the agenda and agree their order and time allocation. Ask members if they want to make any changes in the agenda.

- Decide how decisions will be made (voting/consensus) and decide on any necessary criteria against which possible decisions should be judged.

During the meeting
See 'Controlling a meeting' below.

Conclude the meeting
- Thank the participants for having achieved the objectives within the time limit.

- Summarize what has been agreed. Make sure that everyone knows who is going to do what, when and where, and have this recorded in the minutes.

- Set the date for the next meeting.

Follow-through
- Ensure that the minutes are distributed.

- Keep in touch with the committee re 'homework' between meetings and preparation for future meetings.

Controlling a meeting

Business involves people working together to get things done as speedily and as effectively as possible. In controlling a meeting, your objective is to reach group assent in minimum time.

- Encourage good communications between participants. Keep an 'open climate' by listening to all contributions (majority and minority), and draw together points of agreement rather than letting people concentrate on differences.

- Observe the time limit for each item on the agenda in order to maintain progress through the agenda. You may need to control individual contributions if time is limited. Avoid choking off discussion before it naturally ends.

- Wait until you get the feeling of the meeting that the time has come for a particular item to be wound up. If the discussion is going round in circles, you should call for a proposal for action.

- Keep people to the point by referring to the agreed plan/agreed limits of the discussion.

- Restrain the over-talkative. Ensure that all interested parties have a chance to speak. Try to bring silent members into the discussion by asking them for their views.

- Allow only one person to speak at a time.

- Allow constructive criticism of proposals. Prohibit personal attacks.

- Ask questions to break through vague and general statements (what? when? where? how? who? why?).

- Summarize progress from time to time. Reviewing the issues that have been agreed up to that time will help to emphasize a sense of progress.

- Consensus versus voting? In general, try to achieve a consensus of opinion, but don't be afraid to call for a vote if the group is badly split on an issue. In striving for consensus, your aim is to identify in what direction the majority view is heading, and then get the minority to accept that this is the view that should prevail.

Reaching a consensus

The main reason for consensus decision making in groups is to avoid splitting the group into 'winners' and 'losers'. It also avoids rigid thinking when there may be other ways of looking at a problem. An insistence on voting can often foster argument rather than rational discussion, and consequently harm the group process.

Consensus, on the other hand, is reached when individual objections or reservations are withdrawn after the competing views have been aired. The group reaches the point where each person can say, 'Well, even though it may not be exactly what I want, at least I can accept the decision and support it'.

You should bear the following in mind when trying to bring about consensus:

- Let true consensus take its time. Early, quick and easy compromises should be avoided.

- Encourage members to state their views in turn rather than through arguments.

- Encourage members to listen to and to focus on what others have to say.

- Try to get any underlying assumptions and views regarding the situation out into the open where they can be discussed.

- Encourage members to consider more aspects of the problem, to treat differences of opinion as a way of gathering additional information and as a means of clarifying issues; differences force the group to seek better information.

- Avoid counting numbers in favour/against proposals.

Participation at meetings

If meetings are to be successful, each person has his or her own distinctive part to play in making the meeting a success. You will find in this guide a number of different roles described. Each person attending the meeting may play one or more roles. It is important that all the roles are performed at some stage of the meeting.

The second part of this guide deals with some of the different behaviours which contribute to the success of a meeting.

Roles people play
There are a number of different roles which contribute to the effectiveness of meetings and other group activities:

- *Chairperson:* responsible for ensuring the progress of the meeting and for following procedures.

- *Shaper:* influences by his or her proposals and by strong argument.

- *Informer:* brings suggestions and/or new information to the meeting.

- *Team worker:* is supportive to others and seeks to defuse conflict.

- *Devil's advocate:* tests the validity of proposals by arguing against them.

- *Assessor:* assesses compliance with group values and norms as well as monitoring progress against objectives.

- *Finisher:* works for progress through the agenda and for closure on items.

Positive behaviours

When you attend meetings, you can play your part by use of the following behaviours as appropriate:

- Encourage people to participate and bring in silent members by asking them for their views.

- Clarify the discussion by looking for examples, and by asking for and giving further information.

- Build on good points made by others.

- Create harmony by mediating differences.

- Summarize the discussion from time to time to demonstrate progress.

- Use humour or call for a break at the right time to ease tension.

- Suggest new ideas for discussion and new approaches to problem solving.

- Admit your difficulty in understanding some issues – others will surely appreciate it.

- Clarify options for the group and make recommendations.

- Test occasionally whether the group is ready to come to a decision.

Assessing a meeting

Most people when they assess a meeting concentrate on the content. Were the main objectives achieved? Were all the topics covered? If you are assessing a meeting, consider process as well as content. Did the people attending contribute fully? Are they satisfied with the outcome?

- Did all the committee members participate?

- Did the group establish criteria for making decisions?

- Were questions asked to break through vague, general statements?

- Did members seek facts/opinions?

- How well was the time managed?

- Did participants really listen to one another?

- Were the objectives spelt out and adhered to?

- Was time allowed for recapping and summarizing?

- What helped or hindered the reaching of solutions?

- Were good points built on?

- How open/defensive were the participants at the meeting?

- Did the group stop from time to time in order to consider how well they were doing, and to discuss what obstacles (if any) interfered with their progress? This is known as 'Group maintenance'.

- You should also consider the non-verbal behaviour in order to sense how participants were feeling about issues.

- Finally, in judging a meeting, remember that problems will always arise when you have a group of people working together. Invariably the following will appear among such problems:

  - identity (why am I here?).

  - power (how much power have I here?).

  - goals (are they clear?).

  - intimacy (how open should I be?).

  - assertiveness (some people might be silent, some over-talkative).

- In summary, how do the participants feel about
  (a) the process of the meeting,
  (b) the content,
  (c) the decisions made, and
  (d) their involvement and treatment during the meeting?

Preparing minutes

Minutes are an important record of the business done at meetings. They should be written up as early as possible after the meeting when you can still remember in detail what has occurred.

- Identify the meeting (the date, time, venue).

- Mention the name of the person in the chair.

- Record the attendance (names of those present and apologies for absence).

- Record the decisions reached. Give the exact wording, and where relevant the names of the movers and seconders and the numbers voting for and against. In an action column alongside each minute include the initials of the person(s) responsible for taking action.

- It is sometimes worthwhile checking the content of the minutes with another committee member to ensure accuracy.

- Avoid the temptation to bias the minutes in favour of your own views.

- Have the minutes ready for approval at the next meeting.

Leading a discussion group

A discussion group is a useful kind of informal, ad hoc meeting. It draws a number of people together to address a specific problem, to consider a situation or to come to a decision. Formalities are kept to a minimum:

- Five to eight people is the ideal number.

- Clarify the objectives of the discussion group.

- Explain how the session will be run.

- Outline the topic for discussion. If necessary, explain its importance.

- Use open questions to keep the discussion moving.

- Write up discussion points/headings on a flip chart.

- Keep participants to the topic.

- Draw out silent members.

- Summarize overall conclusions.

A conference checklist

The following checklist will prove useful when you are organizing that special conference.

- *When to hold it*
  What is the exact date and time of the conference? Does the date clash with important national, local, business or calendar events? Does it clash with any major planned maintenance work?

- *Venue*
  Will it be an external venue or the company's conference room? What hotel or restaurant is normally used for this type of conference? Has it been satisfactory? Has the availability of the venue been checked? Are there any noisy roadworks, etc., nearby?

- *Participants/staff*
  Who will be attending? Are the key people available? Will people arrange their own accommodation? Does anyone else need to know of the intended conference? Are conference staff required? How many? What are their roles? Who is in overall charge?

- *Guest speakers*
  Will the guest speakers be expected to look after their own travel arrangements and accommodation. Do they know how to get to the venue? Have you advised the guest speakers in writing of the arrangements, and have you received confirmation from them of their intention to attend? Have you arranged that relevant needs of the guest speakers (such as visual aids) will be met satisfactorily? When will guest speakers be able to set up their visual aids? Will they need help with these? Will the guest speakers be present all day? Have you appointed a liaison person to look after the guest speakers?

- *Conference room*
  What layout and seating arrangements will be required? Will you

need a seating plan? When can the layout be physically implemented (chairs, tables, visual aids, folders, water jugs and glasses, etc.), and who will do it? Do all the lights work? Is there backup equipment? Is heating and ventilation satisfactory? Are there enough suitably positioned and matching power points for conference equipment? Will there be enough room for speakers to move about easily? What will happen if there is a power cut, etc.? Do you require name plates for participants? What about a notice for the outside of the conference room to advise people not to interrupt?

- *Paperwork*
  Do participants require folders, paper, pens, etc.? Are the speakers' scripts available for distribution? Who is responsible for conference stationery?

- *Breaks*
  What are the times of lunch and refreshments breaks? Will transport be required at lunchtime? Have the catering arrangements for the breaks been made? Who will organize ventilation and servicing of the room during breaks?

- *Messages*
  Will you need to tell the switchboard operator not to interrupt? How will delegates know about messages? Where will they be kept? Are telephone, facsimile, telex facilities available?

- *Budget*
  Does anything need to be purchased or ordered in advance? What is the budget position? Who pays for drinks? Is the menu fixed choice? What will be the total cost? What are the arrangements for paying the bill?

- *Recording*
  Will the conference be recorded (audio, video, note-taking)? Who is responsible?

- *Clean up*
  Who is responsible for tidying up after the conference?

- *Wrap up*
  Who is responsible for implementing conference decisions? How will that be done? Who will deal with 'thank you' letters, fees and expenses for conference staff and speakers?

9   Communication

Your ability to interact with others, both within and outside your organization, plays a critical role in your effectiveness as a manager. The way in which you interact is by communicating. Research indicates that most managers spend 70% of their time communicating with superiors, peers and subordinates. Clearly, they must possess good communication skills if they are to be effective.

Of course, there are born communicators just as there are people naturally gifted in most skills areas. However, communication skills can be learned by identifying and trying out the best practices. In this section there are guides to a range of communication skills including assertion, non-verbal behaviour, listening and writing. The section begins by identifying the barriers to effective communication, and by setting out seven rules for effective communication. You can use these rules to test the effectiveness of all your communications.

There are two themes common to all the guides. Firstly, the communicated message succeeds to the extent to which it takes into account the disposition of the person(s) to whom it is addressed. Secondly, no communication process is complete unless the communicator receives feedback regarding the impact of the message. Feedback not only tells whether the message has been understood and accepted. It also informs the communicator as to the effectiveness of his or her communication skills.

Managing the communication process

Even a quick flick through this guide will show you how important communication is to the work of the manager. Managers communicate with superiors and subordinates. They communicate with customers and with suppliers. They communicate to give information and to receive information. They communicate by speaking, listening, writing and reading. They communicate by their actions and by observing what others do. Yet the amount of communication is so great and the barriers to good communication are so many that managers must develop a great number of skills if they are to be effective communicators.

Think of communication as a six-stage process. Each stage must be successfully managed if a communication is to be effective.

- *Develop the message*
  Make sure what what you want to communicate is properly reflected in the communication. Are you clear about what you want to say, what information you must supply, what outcomes you are looking for?

- *Prepare the communication*
  Decide what method of communication you will use. Do you need to use more than one method? For example, face to face communication is best for influencing people, but written communications are best for dealing with detailed information.

- *Transmit the information*
  When and where should you meet with the person for face to face discussion? Should the written message be by letter, telex or a facsimile transmission. There is a routine in most organizations for

transmitting information. You should take the time to consider which is the most appropriate method.

- *Reception*
  Think about how the message will be received. Will everyone be at the meeting? Will your message arrive on time? Do people read memos? If not, your message will not be received.

- *Reaction to the message*
  This is the most important stage. You want the receiver to take action, otherwise there was no point in the communication. It depends on two factors, the ability and the disposition of the receiver.

  Much organizational communication is prepared in a technical way – for example, marketing forecasts, financial analyses or engineering reports – which the receiver may be unable to understand. The receiver's disposition (such as hostility or indifference) may make him or her unwilling to take positive action as a result of the communication. Many memos sent in organizations are simply ignored.

- *Feedback*
  Check with the receiver to ensure that the communication has been understood and acted upon. Any communication process which does not include a feedback loop is of little value, since the sender doesn't know whether the message has been understood and acted upon in the right way.

Planning your communication

Use the following checklist so that the right information reaches the right people to take the right action. Prepare a plan for effective communication.

- What is the objective of the communication? If you are not clear about that, what chance has the receiver?

- To whom is the communication addressed? You weaken the impact of your communication if you repeatedly communicate to people who are not directly involved.

- Be certain what action you want the receiver to take. This must be clear in the communication.

- Set a time for completion of the communication process.

- What barriers to effective communication apply in this case? Review the barriers to communication and make a list of the key ones.

- What tactics will you employ to overcome these barriers, and to overcome resistance to action on the part of the receiver?

- What information must be included in the communication? What are the main points you want to make? Are they clearly set out? What data or support information should you supply?

- What communications media should you use? For complex messages a variety of media is required, such as face-to-face followed up by a written message.

- How will you determine that the information has been understood?

- How will you be certain that the information has been acted on?

Barriers to communication

Determine how some of the more significant barriers to communication will affect you. Go through the list and prepare a tactic for avoiding each barrier.

- *Language*
  If the communication is to be successful, the sender must prepare the message in the language of the receiver. Highly technical scientific reports are unlikely to influence professionals from other areas, such as accountants, to commit themselves to some action.

- *Noise*
  The term 'noise' refers to anything which interferes with or degrades communications in organizations. For example, your message is competing with other messages for attention. If the receiver gets loads of memos each day, you should look at some other way of sending your message.

- *Too many steps*
  Most people have heard of the army command which started at one end of the trench as 'send reinforcements, we are going to advance', and ended at the other end as 'send three and fourpence, we are going to a dance'. Use the least number of steps in your communications.

- *Listening difficulties*
  There are many listening difficulties for the receiver. Pressure of work, other priorities or overload of communications are all causes of listening difficulties.

- *Distrust*
  There are many reasons why the receiver may distrust or be cynical about a communication. Some of the distrust may be caused by the sender – for instance, if you mark all your correspondence

'urgent', or if you have been less than candid in earlier communications.

- *Emotions*
  Emotions affect communications in two ways. Firstly, an emotionally charged situation generates a great deal of noise which distorts the communication. Secondly, the most effective means of achieving action action from someone else is through their emotions. This component is at work when you sell the benefits rather than the features of a proposal.

- *Feedback loop*
  Absence of a feedback loop prevents the sender from being sure that his or her message has been fully understood.

Seven rules for effective communication

- *Prepare a communication plan*
- Clarify the objectives of your communication. What are you trying to achieve? What information are you trying to transmit? What action do you want the other party to take?

- *Focus on the receiver*
  How will your message motivate the receiver to take the action you desire? Consult with others. If you want to check that your message will be understood, try out your message with others. You will be surprised at how often a message which was clear to you is not understood by others.

- *Clear the airways*
  Overcome the problem of noise by clearing the airways of other messages or by developing a new channel for communication, such as an after hours meeting.

- *Manage distrust*
  Overcome distrust by being open, warm, supportive and trusting in your own communications. Help the receiver to interpret what you are saying and spell out the advantages and disadvantages of your proposal. Make it clear that you will listen to what the other party has to say.

- *Act consistently with your communication*
  Messages come from actions more loudly than from words – for example, don't call an important meeting and then send a deputy. Don't dictate a letter of apology and ask your secretary to sign it.

- *Communicate regularly*
  Water dripping on a stone approach is more likely to be effective than an occasional flood of communications.

- *Listen carefully*

  By far the most effective forms of communication are two way rather than one way. Carefully listening to the other party's needs, cares and understanding with regard to your communication greatly increases its chance of success.

Being assertive

Being assertive means standing up for your own rights while respecting the rights of the person to whom you are speaking. You communicate exactly what is on your mind, but do so in a way which demonstrates regard for the other person. You feel good as a person when you are assertive since you are not allowing yourself to be pushed around. It is an important skill to have socially as well as at work. Being assertive enables you to express your views strongly to your manager and work colleagues without causing friction. Outside of work you will find it easier to deal with queue jumpers and with people who give you bad service.

There are three postures in communication. You can be diffident, assertive or aggressive. Diffidence shows a lack of confidence in your own position. Aggression shows a lack of regard for the other person's position. Assertion allows you to show self-confidence combined with a regard for the other person's position. Your posture will be clear from your body language as well as from the words you use.

Body language
- The diffident communicator speaks in a low, apologetic and hesitant voice. Eye contact is avoided and if the hands are not clasped together, they tend to be used to cover the mouth or face.

- The loud, staccato voice of the aggressive communicator is accompanied by unfriendly gestures such as a clenched fist, banging the table and a forward leaning body. When eye contact is made, the eyes glare.

- The assertive communicator maintains fairly constant eye contact and speaks in a firm and clear voice. The body is relaxed and gestures are open and friendly.

Language

- Diffident communicators use tentative language containing phrases and expressions such as 'maybe', 'should we', 'I wonder if', 'perhaps'. They will often belittle the importance of their own points.

- Aggressive communications are characterized by warnings, sarcasm, abrupt remarks and contradictions. Criticisms tend to be directed against people rather than the situation or problem.

- The language of the assertive communicator focuses on the situation and the problem. The words 'I' and 'you' occur frequently. Verbs are used in the present tense. 'What I want you to do is . . .'.

Formula for assertiveness

Use the "DESC" formula for assertiveness:

D – *Describe* the problem.
E – What *effect* has this problem on you?
S – *Specify* the action you want the other person to take.
C – If appropriate or necessary, tell the person the *consequences* of failure to act.

Before using this formula make sure that you have the other person's full attention. If he or she fails to respond, use the broken record technique, that is, keep repeating your point until it is acknowledged. Be sure to acknowledge the points made by the other party. The best way to do this is to reflect them back. 'What you are saying is . . .'.

One final point. Assertiveness greatly improves the effectiveness of your communications, and maintains your self-esteem, but it is irritating to other people if you are assertive all the time. Be prepared to compromise occasionally.

Non-verbal behaviour

Research carried out on non-verbal behaviour usually claims that the facial expressions and gestures of a speaker (anger, disgust, fear, interest, joy, sadness, surprise, etc.) are many times more powerful than the words used. An appreciation of how to read body language is a useful skill to have in your communication skills repertoire. Don't overdo the analysis, however, and jump to conclusions, such as reading meaning where none exists. Remember also that your own non-verbals are observed by others.

- Notice people's posture. People generally move closer to those they like and trust and away from those they fear or distrust. Also when people are getting on well together, their postures are generally similar. They mirror each other's body language. They give each other non-verbal encouragement through nodding their heads in approval, smiling.

- Listen to the tone of voice to catch the underlying feelings behind words.

- When you listen to people, look at them quite frequently. This conveys enthusiasm and liking. Leaning forward in your chair also indicates interest.

- Don't cover your mouth with your hand. It betrays uncertainty.

- Notice how people manage their space; where they stand in a lift; how they impress their own personality in their work space.

- Some other signs to observe are: clenched fist, banging on the table, drumming with the fingers (anger or irritation); rubbing the nose (puzzled); shrugging the shoulders (indifference); hugging the body, that is, arms tightly folded and legs crossed (feeling threatened);

slumped shoulders (expecting defeat); poor eye contact (lack of sincerity).

- Look for clusters of behaviours. Don't rely on a single piece of body language.

Developing verbal fluency

Managers are expected to be fluent speakers, but they, like everyone else, can find themselves fumbling for words on occasions. Here are some exercises for verbal fluency. They will develop your ability to think quickly.

- Look at the 'Letters to the Editor' section of your newspaper and pick a subject heading that appeals to you. Read the letter aloud and then speak your views on it, agree or disagree and give your reasons accordingly.

- Do likewise for the editorial in the newspaper and for one or two of the main news items. It can help your fluency if you imagine that a TV or radio interviewer has just said to you 'Can you tell me in the one minute remaining to us what your views are on . . .' (the news item you have selected from your newspaper).

- Look round the room and select an object at random. Observe it closely and write down all the ideas that occur to you about that object, no matter how trivial. When you have listed a number of ideas, look at the first idea on your list and speak about it in the words that come to mind. When the flow of words ceases, go on to the second idea and so on down your list.

- Make a tour of your house and examine the pictures on the walls. Describe the pictures and the meaning they have for you.

- Close your eyes and imagine that you are conducting a group on a speaking tour of your house.

- List three things that happened to you today and speak aloud on these.

- Buy a book of quotations and use the quotations for fluency practice as follows. Pick a quotation and write out the outline thoughts it suggests to you. Then practise speaking aloud on the written outline for a minute or two. When the time is up, round off what you have been saying with a definite conclusion.

Do one of these exercises once a day, for example at home or in your car, and hear your fluency increase.

Listening

The key to influencing is listening. It requires effort. Because our span of attention is very short, the tendency is to drift in and out of listening. The following hints will help you to be a more active listener and, consequently, a more effective influencer of people. Listening can be divided into two categories: empathetic listening and critical listening.

Empathetic listening
This kind of listening motivates the speaker to speak in a more open way, because he or she knows you are listening sympathetically.

- Let the speaker know that you will give him or her the time to say his or her piece.

- Delay any evaluation until you have heard all the story. Wait out the person's pauses.

- Use eye-contact and give verbal and non-verbal encouragement as appropriate; for instance, 'I see, I understand', nodding, smiling, etc.

- Do not fake understanding. Ask the person to explain.

- Mentally record/summarize the main points the person is making.

- Repeat the message back to the person in order to show you understand; 'I understand you to mean that . . .'.

- Watch the person's body language for clues to their meaning (facial expression, body movements, posture).

Critical listening
In critical listening you evaluate critically the ideas and arguments presented. Lawyers and debaters, for example, look for contradictions,

irrelevancies, errors and weaknesses in their opponent's case. In using critical listening, ask yourself:

- Whom does the speaker represent?

- Are claims supported/documented?

- Is credibility demonstrated?

- Is he or she speaking in generalities? Insist that the speaker move from generalities to specifics.

- Use probing and leading questions to challenge what has been said.

- Being a critical listener is not the same as being hostile. Try to be critical without upsetting the speaker.

- Concentrate on the facts, not on discrediting the speaker.

Do's and don'ts for better writing

Most managers learn how to write at school. However, the essay style is not suitable for business writing. These guidelines will make your writing easier to read and to understand. Also, people will be more likely to want to read your memos, reports, etc.

Do

- explain any technical terms your use;

- use the person's name and the magic word 'you';

- use charts, graphs and illustrations;

- use the journalists' approach. Tell them what you are going to tell them, tell them, then tell them what you told them;

- use short sentences and paragraphs;

- try to keep letters and memos to a single page.

Don't

- use a long word where a short word will do;

- write in the third person if you can avoid it;

- write long complicated sentences;

- clutter up your text with unnecessary information and tables of data. Put them in appendices;

- produce lengthy documents or bulky reports which busy colleagues will not read.

Report writing

Report writing is an essential skill for managers. The best reports lead to action. The others become dust collectors. How you prepare your report will determine how top management and your colleagues respond to it. Bear in mind how managers read reports.

- The most common framework for a report is:

  - Terms of reference.

  - Procedure adopted.

  - Findings.

  - Conclusions.

  - Recommendations.

  These terms are explained in Guide 9.

- In writing your report avoid jargon; prefer the active voice to the passive voice; keep your words/sentences/paragraphs short. For variety, balance your sentences by having some a little longer.

- If the report is confidential, indicate this on the cover. The cover, or title page, also includes a brief descriptive title, the name of the author, the date of compilation and a list of the names of the people receiving the report.

- Before submitting your report check spelling and layout carefully. Also check consistency of abbreviations and symbols. Number the pages. Are your recommendations clear? Are they justified, and based on sound facts/evidence? Have you defined technical terms?

- Put complicated supporting data in the appendices rather than in the main body of the report.

- In a long report you will need to include (apart from the above headings) a table of contents, and a brief summary (usually one page) of the main recommendations. This appears at the beginning of the report. Reserve any lengthy details for the appendices. If you include an introduction, it should set out the essential background and include the objectives of the report, the terms of reference, why the report was requested and by whom. Mention earlier reports if relevant.

How managers read reports
Only a minority of managers bother to work diligently through all the documents they receive. A recent study shows how managers read reports:

Summary of recommendations	100% of the time
Introduction	68% of the time
Body of the report	22% of the time
Conclusions	55% of the time
Appendices	15% of the time

Bear this in mind when you are writing your next report.

The elements of a report

The usual headings of a report are given below, with some explanations and useful phrases as a lead-in to these items in your report.

Terms of reference
Terms of reference state the authority on which you are acting, and they contain a statement of formal submission. For example, 'I have been asked by the Managing Director to examine and report on the main causes of accidents to machine operators in the tool room during the period February 1st–April 30th of last year. I now submit my report'.

It is important to stick to your terms of reference despite the temptation to depart from them. Keep them in front of you as you develop your report.

Procedure adopted
Mention the sources from which your facts/evidence are derived and upon which your conclusions are based. Here is an example: 'The conclusions on page . . . were based on information derived from –

1 Interviews with
   • Managing Director.
   • Heads of departments.
   • Supervisors.
   • Machine operators.

2 Analysis of accident records
   • Period June–July 1988.
   • Period June–July 1989.
   • Comparison of 1988 with 1989.

3 Comparison with other companies in the industry.

Findings

The body of the report is concerned with your findings, what you discovered from your sources, the facts. List your findings under appropriate headings. Bear in mind the importance of simplicity. Remove any lengthy sections from the main body of the report and place them in appendices.

In your main text you might refer to an appendix as follows: 'Figures in Appendix 3 show that our accident rate was much higher in June–July 1991 than in June–July 1990. The reasons for the increase were . . .'.

Conclusions

Lay out each conclusion clearly and give each a separate line or paragraph. For example, 'Based on the findings, my conclusions are as follows:

(1) . . .   (2) . . .'.

When giving conclusions you may need to suggest that further meetings and/or more detailed information are needed.

Recommendations

Write strong recommendations and link them to the conclusions of the report; 'Based on the conclusions set out above, my recommendations are as follows.

(1) That . . .   (2) That . . .   (3) That . . .

Appendices

Include in the appendices items such as: the results of experiments; statistical data; tables and graphs; reports, correspondence; worked examples; costings.

Selling your report

Reports are notorious for being unread and locked away in desk drawers. Consider 'selling' your report. You did, after all, put a great deal of energy into writing it.

- When handing in your report, take people through it and explain any important issues.

- Issue summary sections on key aspects of the report.

- Publish progress reports on what is happening to your document.

- Be sure to include the costs and benefits of each recommendation.

- Make sure that it is on the agenda of various organization meetings and is discussed systematically and in depth.

- Include a covering letter which mentions why people should read the report and support it.

- Follow up your report through personal contact.

- A formal verbal presentation will help you to sell your report. In fact, a combination of the written report with a verbal presentation is becoming standard practice.

- In preparing your verbal presentation, ask yourself what objections you expect to your recommendations. How do you propose dealing with these objections?

Writing a business letter

Business writing is an important managerial skill that is often under-valued. It is frequently regarded as a chore, yet most managers spend at least 10% of their working day in some form of writing. It is a skill that requires effort and understanding more than inspiration. Here are some guidelines:

- Write with your audience in mind and adjust your language to what is most meaningful for your reader. Put yourself in the reader's place.

- Keep your writing clear, simple and natural. Know what you want to achieve. Keep it conversational, that is, use words and phrases from your everyday speaking vocabulary. Use the active rather than passive voice.

- Use short words, short sentences, short paragraphs. However, occasionally vary sentence length for variety.

- Space your writing for eye-appeal and use attention-getting devices such as underlining, capitalization, indenting, etc.

- Avoid jargon and technical terms that may not be clear to your reader.

- In a persuasive letter, promise a benefit and enlarge on it. Tell the reader specifically what benefit he or she will receive. Back up your benefit statement with relevant proof.

- Tell the reader what he or she might lose if they don't act *now*.

- Remember the ABC of writing – Always Be Courteous.

Writing a letter of complaint

Sometimes you have to write a letter of complaint to another organization such as a supplier.

- Make the complaint specific. Avoid vague complaints and generalizations.

- Make sure your facts are correct.

- Mention the good points of the product/service thereby showing tact and balance.

- Express regret at having to complain to a company of such repute. Say the complaint on this occasion is too serious to be overlooked.

- Be explicit about the action you expect.

- Ask for a speedy response to your complaint.

Replying to complaints

Here is a good approach, if you have to reply to a letter of complaint received by your company:

- Begin the letter with an expression of regret.

- Avoid the temptation to win an argument.

- Explain the circumstances which caused the trouble or difficulty. Don't be over-defensive.

- Express the hope that the other party is not unduly inconvenienced.

- Say exactly what you are going to do to set matters right.

- Don't over-commit your company, if the customer is partly to blame.

- Say that every effort will be made to prevent a recurrence.

- End the letter by hoping for a continuation of good relations between the company and the customer.

10   Presentation

Most people have a great fear of public speaking. In fact, in a recent survey, speaking to an audience was placed ahead of death as the greatest fear of all. The apprehension seems to increase when the audience is well known to the speaker. People feel particularly exposed when giving a talk to colleagues and to friends. And yet managers today are increasingly called upon to make presentations as a means of having their ideas and proposals considered by colleagues. They are often called upon to represent their organizations at public events where they are expected to be perceived as professional and competent presenters.

There is no more frustrating experience than failing to have a good idea or proposal accepted because of an inability to project one's message successfully. All the time and effort spent on a project can come to nought if you are not able to persuade others to your point of view. Not only is the project endangered, but your own personal stature is at risk when you make a presentation. For this most important reason a whole section of this manual has been devoted to becoming a successful presenter.

Practice is the secret to success in presentation skills more than any other skill dealt with in this manual. But practice is of little value if your technique is defective. In fact, many experienced presenters continue to be ineffective despite years of experience. The guides in this section will enable you to use the most effective techniques as you practise your presentation skills.

The first couple of guides deal with collecting information, preparing the presentation, preparing yourself and creating a structure for the presentation. Too often, during preparation,there is an undue emphasis on the content with only a negative attitude to the people involved – worry for oneself and anxiety about the attitude of the audience to oneself. A much more positive approach is required – an approach which emphasizes what you can do to help yourself and to win the hearts and minds of the audience.

The next group of guides deals with your delivery of the presentation, including the use of visual aids and, in particular, the overhead projector. Good techniques in these areas can greatly enhance the professionalism of the presentation and your perceived competence as a presenter.

Finally, there are a set of guides which provides a framework for many of the informal or social presentations which you may be required to give from time to time. They are usually prepared on the back of an envelope and they usually come across as having been inadequately prepared. Use these guides so that you will always present yourself at your best.

Preparing a presentation

Preparation has often been called 'the mother of confidence'. If your presentation is well prepared, with a definite aim in mind, and well rehearsed, it will be a successful one. Here are some general points to bear in mind when you are under the spotlight:

- Decide whether you are going to use a fully written script or just headings, for example on numbered cards, to act as prompts and reminders.

- If you use a full script, make it easier for yourself to deliver by having short sentences, short paragraphs and short words. Leave plenty of 'vacant' space on the paper.

- Always know word for word how you are going to open and conclude your presentation. You want to create strong first and last impressions.

- Avoid jargon, and make sure you explain any technical terms used. Avoid getting bogged down in details. You might consider saying, for example, 'I've left out the detail on this matter but you'll find it in the script/full report'.

- Rehearse, rehearse, rehearse – with your notes and your visual aids. Most presentations are poor because they have not been sufficiently rehearsed.

- The best rehearsals are out loud. But you can use waiting time at work, at the airport or on a train, etc., to go over it in your mind. Put it on a tape and play it over in your car.

- Before the presentation begins, use deep breathing to relax yourself. Breathe in through your nose until your abdomen is filled. Hold your breath for a count of five, then exhale.

- Inspect the room beforehand to ensure that all the facilities you need are in working order.

- Imagine that you are giving the presentation and that it is a great success. Athletes use this technique to put themselves into a positive frame of mind.

The magic envelope technique

This is a technique to help you write articles, presentations and reports.

- Take a large envelope and on its outside write two dates. One of these is the date on which you have to make your presentation. The other date is called your 'Convergent thinking day', that is, the day on which you will sort and put a logical structure on whatever material you have put into your envelope during the divergent thinking part of your preparation. Be careful that you don't leave your convergent writing to the last minute.

- Leave your envelope on your desk or in some other conspicuous spot. In doing so, the envelope will stimulate your subconscious mind to think creatively about your writing.

- Begin at once to write notes for the envelope, no matter what. It might be your own 'off the top of your head' views on the subject. Write these out on a page or two of paper and put them into your envelope. It is important to start your own creative flow before you rush off to do any necessary research.

- As the creative process quickens, other pieces of information will find their way into your envelope. It will be bulging with: your on-going random thoughts on the subject; clippings from newspapers or magazines; various bits of information collected; reports of interviews carried out; statistics; relevant quotes; diagrams; charts; photographs; analysis of records, etc.

- One piece of paper will have an answer to this key question: what do I hope to achieve with this presentation: what's my objective? Other pieces of paper will have question headings such as: what are my terms of reference and what exactly have I been asked to talk about?

Am I required to make recommendations? Who is my audience? What's in it for them? What action do I want my audience to take?

- When the convergent thinking day arrives, take a close look at the material in your envelope. Edit your material. Put a logical structure on your bits and pieces. Be ruthless in your selection. Avoid getting bogged down in too much detail. Aim for simplicity.

- Attempt a first draft. Never let this first draft out of your hands. Good writing is not written, it is re-written.

- The magic envelope technique is equally effective for preparing reports and articles.

Presenting at short notice

This four-stage formula is most effective in attracting and keeping the interest of audiences. Use it to structure your presentations. It is particularly valuable when you have to prepare a presentation at short notice. Divide a sheet of paper into four boxes. Scribble notes into each box on what you are going to say.

- *Grab attention*
  Many presentations are doomed from the start because of a boring opening. Catch your audience. Tell a joke, ask a question, relate an anecdote or give some highly significant information. Make sure your opening remarks are in keeping with the tone and content of the rest of the presentation.

- *Outline*
  Give the audience an outline of what you are going to say, tell them the purpose of your presentation and why it affects them.

- *Convince*
  In this stage you seek to convince your audience. Present your argument in a logical sequence. You must also take account of your listeners' feelings so that they not only agree with you but want to take action. Do not rely on data alone. Give specific examples or refer to the endorsement of some respected person. Be careful not to dilute your proposal with too many (weak) arguments in favour.

- *Ask for action*
  End your presentation by telling your audience exactly what it is you want them to do; for example, close by 'asking for the order'.

Delivering a presentation

Many well prepared presentations are spoiled by poor delivery. Here are some pointers to bear in mind:

- Practise some deep slow breathing from the stomach region before you begin, to ease any tension you may be feeling.

- Don't be in a hurry to begin. To do so shows nervousness.

- Stand upright in a relaxed position. Balance the weight of your body equally on both feet. Don't slump or cross your legs.

- Know your introduction and your conclusion so well that you can deliver them while maintaining full eye-contact with your audience.

- Let your hands naturally express themselves. Avoid bitty gestures. Expansive gestures demonstrate an open personality.

- Use the occasional pause. Vary your rate of speaking and emphasize key words in order to avoid a monotonous delivery.

- Don't bury your head in your notes. Be so familiar with them through rehearsal that you can maintain maximum eye contact with your audience.

- Look at individual members of your audience. When you do this, let your eyes rest on them for a few seconds each time you come to look at them.

Closing a presentation

The close of a presentation is of vital importance. Leave your audience with a good final impression of you. In one or two memorable sentences draw together and round-off the various points you have developed throughout your presentation. Bring audience interest to a climax and motivate the desired response. Here are some ways of doing this.

- Give a summary of your main points; for instance, 'We have seen (1) . . . (2) . . . (3) These, therefore, are the reasons why . . .'.

- End with a relevant quotation.

- Tell a relevant story which sums up your message.

- Pose a question for your audience to think about.

- Write three or four words on a flipchart which serves as a visual summing-up of your presentation, such as 'More calls mean more sales'.

- Never conclude by saying, 'That's all I have to say'. Always have a definite conclusion. Know it word for word and you will be able to have final eye-contact with your audience. It is a touch of courtesy to your audience to finish with the words 'Thank you'.

- The strongest ending asks the audience to take some specific action.

Visual aids

There is an old Arab proverb which says that a great orator has the ability to turn the ears of the audience into eyes. Visual aids can help you to do the same thing.

- Your visual aids can be newspaper clippings; books/magazines; wall charts; pie-charts; maps; graphs; bar-charts; flow diagrams; tables; cartoons; pictograms; flip-charts; models (static or working); slides; relevant objects.

- Don't use a written aid that is too detailed or crowded. Use few words, easy to see and read at a distance.

- As you prepare and rehearse your presentation, link in the visual aids and know exactly how and where you are going to use them.

- Keep your visual aids out of sight until you are ready to use them.

- Avoid turning your back on your audience when using visual aids.

- Keep quiet for a moment to let your audience read a slide before you comment on it.

- Visual aids can distract an audience so put them out of sight when your point is made.

A formula for using visual aids

Here is a useful formula for using visual aids in a presentation. The examples given relate to graphs, but the formula works for most visual aids.

- Use a transition statement as a lead-in to the graph; for example, 'The graph to my right illustrates our production figures for the first quarter of this year'.

- Describe the key elements of the visual aid; 'Note that the vertical axis depicts the quantity of production. The horizontal axis covers the weeks from the first of January'.

- Make your main point; 'You can see that output is down in January, that is more or less expected but as we move into February things begin to pick up. In March, production really takes off due to increased productivity'.

- Then make a transition to your next point; 'How do I see the outlook for the rest of the year? Well, based on sales forecasts . . .'.

- Remove the visual aid from view when you have made your point and the audience has assimilated its contents.

Using the overhead projector

The great advantage of an overhead projector is that it enables you to face your audience all the time while you are making your presentation. In addition, no blackout facilities are required.

- Check that it is available and working before the meeting. Make sure your acetates can be seen by everyone in the audience.

- Switch the OHP off when not in use so that the audience's attention returns from the screen to you.

- When displaying a list of items, use the gradual disclosure technique. You cover the list with a piece of paper and slowly move it down the list to give the information incrementally. This technique arouses curiosity about what is still unrevealed but prevents the audience reading ahead. Don't overuse it, though.

- Emphasize key words by resting a pointer such as a pencil on these words. Move the pointer slowly because the projector 'speeds up' your hand movements.

- The use of overlays – placing one acetate on top of another – enables you to give information dramatically.

- When preparing acetates by hand, use capital letters. It is better to use computer generated graphics. Audiences expect them nowadays.

- If using a photocopier to prepare your acetates, use coloured acetates for background contrast.

- Try not to have more than six lines of text per acetate and no more than six words per line.

- Consider photocopying the acetates to use as handouts after the presentation.

- Increase the visual impact of your acetates by using colour (for contrast), pictures/cartoons (for humour), graphs, boxing and underlining.

Introducing a speaker

If you have to introduce a speaker, here is a format to be followed:

- Welcome the speaker and announce the title of the talk.

- Mention the subject's relevance.

- Mention the speaker's qualifications and experience.

- Point out any link the speaker might have with, for example, the organization, the town or the audience.

- Briefly describe the speaker's other interests (if relevant).

- Conclude by saying, 'Ladies and Gentlemen, Mr/Mrs/Ms . . .', and lead the applause.

- Be careful in saying these few words (two minutes maximum) that you do not commit the speaker to any particular line of approach. Don't indulge in your own 'pet' views on the subject.

- Keep your introduction compatible with the content and tone of the speaker's talk.

- Check with the speaker beforehand if he or she will take questions at the end of the talk.

Proposing a vote of thanks

You may be called upon to propose a vote of thanks at the end of a presentation.

- Listen carefully to the talk, and as you do so, select and jot down one or two points that appealed to you.

- Build your vote of thanks around these selected points. For example, 'Mr Chairman, Ladies and Gentleman, . . . made two points which particularly appealed to me. First of all . . . Secondly, . . . In conclusion, I found our speaker's presentation very witty, enjoyable and informative and so I'm delighted to propose this vote of thanks'.

- As a general rule, any disagreement with the speaker should be kept out of a vote of thanks.

- Place yourself in a strategic position when giving a vote of thanks, stand in the front so that you have eye-contact with the whole audience. Turn occasionally to the speaker.

Speaking at a company competition

If you have to 'say a few words' at the end of a company competition, you might cover the following:

- Speak of the value of such competitions and the qualities needed for success.

- Say how much you enjoyed judging the competition.

- Point out the merits of the best work.

- Name the winners and make the presentation of the awards.

Opening an event

Companies frequently sponsor events and you may be asked on behalf of your company to open such an event. Here are some pointers:

- Express your pleasure in being asked to open the event.

- Congratulate the organization responsible for organizing the event.

- Describe briefly the organization's work and what it does for the community or for people generally.

- Talk about the occasion and the place. Tell why the organization needs funds and that your company is very pleased to help out. Mention the target if one has been set.

- Mention the various events and be careful not to miss any from your list. However, if there are too many, just mention the general categories.

- Mention the entertainment and the catering arrangements.

- Speak about the co-operation and teamwork that has brought all sections of the community together.

- Finally, wish the event every success and then declare it open.

Presenting an award

If you have to present an award to a member of your staff or to someone outside your company, here is a useful method:

- Mention the reason for the award.

- Elaborate on the person's achievements.

- Describe the award, its meaning, uses, history, etc., where appropriate.

- Make the formal presentation; for example, 'On behalf of . . . I'm delighted to present you with this well-deserved award. Congratulations'.

- Shake the recipient's hand and step back and listen to the recipient's words of acceptance.

The retirement presentation

You may have to make a presentation to a person retiring from your company.

- Say that it is both a happy and a sad occasion. Happy because everyone is here to congratulate . . . on his or her retirement and sad because 'we're sorry to lose you'.

- Mention the person's length of service with the company and some of the changes which have taken place during that time.

- Give a brief biography of the person.

- Highlight some of the person's outstanding achievements or contributions to the company. Refer to things that made him or her 'special'.

- Mention the person's intentions for his or her retirement and emphasize how busy the person will be in his or her new life (avoid the 'well-earned rest' theme).

- Congratulate the person and make the presentation.

Accepting an award

In your career as an achieving manager you will, we hope, be in that pleasant position of having to say a few words when awards are presented to you.

- Express your sincere thanks for the award and for the kind wishes that accompany it.

- Mention by name any other people who have helped you and then thank them specifically.

- Speak of the significance of the award and how much it means to you. Mention the encouragement you feel as a result of the award.

- Possibly display the award and speak of its attractiveness, usefulness, etc. Say what you intend doing with it, for example, where in your home or office you are going to place it.

- Finally, once more express your thanks for the award; 'I shall always cherish this award and what it stands for. Thank you'.

DATE DUE

GAYLORD			PRINTED IN U.S.A.